PRETEND PLAY
WORKSHOP
for kids

PRETEND PLAY WORKSHOP
for kids

A Year of DIY Craft Projects
and Open-Ended Screen-Free
Learning for Kids Ages 3–7

Caitlin Kruse and Mandy Roberson,
Founders of MAGIC playbook
with Emma Johnson, M.S.

QUARRY

Quarto.com

© 2023 Quarto Publishing Group USA Inc.
Text © 2023 Magic Playbook LLC and Emma Johnson

First Published in 2023 by Quarry Books, an imprint of The Quarto Group,
100 Cummings Center, Suite 265-D, Beverly, MA 01915, USA.

Quarry Books titles are also available at discount for retail, wholesale, promotional, and bulk purchase. For details, contact the Special Sales Manager by email at specialsales@quarto.com or by mail at The Quarto Group, Attn: Special Sales Manager, 100 Cummings Center, Suite 265-D, Beverly, MA 01915, USA.

27 26 25 24 23   1 2 3 4 5

ISBN: 978-0-7603-8197-7

Digital edition published in 2023
eISBN: 978-0-7603-8198-4

Library of Congress Cataloging-in-Publication Data

Names: Kruse, Caitlin, author. | Roberson, Amanda, author. | Johnson, Emma
  (Childhood educator), author.
Title: Pretend play workshop for kids : a year of DIY craft projects and
  open-ended screen-free learning for kids ages 3-7 / Caitlin Kruse and
  Amanda Roberson, founders of MAGIC Playbook ; with Emma Johnson, M.Ed.
Description: Beverly, MA, USA : Quarry Books, 2023. | Includes index. |
  Summary: "Pretend Play Workshop for Kids offers a year of screen-free
  dramatic play scenarios for adults to set up and kids to engage with,
  featuring open-ended making and learning"-- Provided by publisher.
Identifiers: LCCN 2023005264 (print) | LCCN 2023005265 (ebook) | ISBN
  9780760381977 (trade paperback) | ISBN 9780760381984 (ebook)
Subjects: LCSH: Creative activities and seat work. | Handicraft.
Classification: LCC LB1537 .K78 2023 (print) | LCC LB1537 (ebook) | DDC
  372.5--dc23/eng/20230222
LC record available at https://lccn.loc.gov/2023005264
LC ebook record available at https://lccn.loc.gov/2023005265

Design and Page Layout: Megan Jones Design
Photography: Raven Vasquez

Printed in China

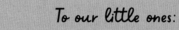

To our little ones:
Brody, Isla, Luca, Piper, Flora, Alice, and Zooey

May you carry the magic of
your childhood with you forever.

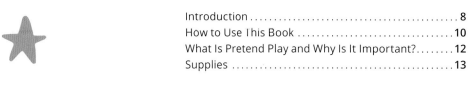

CONTENTS

1

PRETEND PLAY
Detective Office — 15

2

PRETEND PLAY
Post Office — 25

3

PRETEND PLAY
Spaceship — 37

4

PRETEND PLAY
Coffee Shop — 47

5

PRETEND PLAY
Art Museum — 57

6

PRETEND PLAY
Laundry Time — 67

INTRODUCTION

What was your best childhood memory? Think back to those carefree days when you felt pure joy and a smile that you couldn't wipe off of your face. What comes to mind? Maybe you were running through the sprinkler or laughing with a sibling while putting on a puppet show. Or perhaps you built a spaceship out of an old refrigerator box and spent the day pretending to be an astronaut. Little did we know, those days of play that would hush away all of our worries and spark our imagination could also impact our happiness and well-being well into adulthood.

Now, as grown-ups with young children in our lives, we become hyperfocused on making sure our kids are hitting every milestone. We are filled with wonder and worry about who these little people will become and whether they will remember their childhoods fondly. As if the monumental pressures of modern parenthood are not enough, we find ourselves with the constant urge to figure out how to make these few, short, early years with the little ones in our lives as magical as possible.

Looking back on our own childhoods, those simple moments of pure childhood bliss always revolved around play and imagination. Whether we were building forts out of old diaper wipe boxes, setting up pretend zoos for our stuffed animals, or turning our bookshelves into little libraries, these impressions make up many of our fondest memories as kids.

With the busyness of our modern lives and the technology that seems to be everywhere, we are dedicated to bringing back the simple magic of childhood. It can feel that everywhere you look there are activities to sign up for, or lists of skills to master, or expensive toys to buy that will all help your child learn and grow, but we sometimes forget about the magic of downtime to just play pretend. These early years of pretend play set the foundation for a lifetime of creativity, exploration, and social and emotional development.

This desire to bring back the magic of childhood connected the three of us moms—Caitlin and Mandy as creatives with six young children between us, and Emma as a new mom and an expert in early childhood education. We wanted to share easy ways to promote imagination and play in our modern world.

This led us to launch Magic Playbook, our play-based activity brand, and now writing this workbook for you. Whether you're a parent, a grandparent, a teacher, or a caregiver to young children, we see you. We understand the struggles of modern parenthood and we know that pressure you feel to make these years with the young children in your lives extra special.

In this book you'll find twelve easy-to-set-up pretend play scenes. We keep them set up for weeks at a time in our homes. As we've seen with our own children, the reward for taking a few minutes to set up a pretend play scene is priceless. Sometimes our children just need the simple framework of a pretend play scene to spark hours of imaginative play.

Keep this book displayed in your playroom or on your bookshelf within easy reach. You don't need fancy supplies or an artistic touch. We will show you how to set up play scenes with things you already have around your home and teach you how you can help engage your child's learning and imagination within these themes.

We hope this book reminds you that the magic of childhood still exists. You have the power to cultivate it.

Now go have fun and play!

HOW TO USE THIS BOOK

We intend this book to inspire you to create pretend play setups that work for you and your children. Feel free to work through it in the order and pace that works best in your life. You do not need to complete every single setup, activity, and project in the order we present them here; in fact, we encourage you not to! Read through and see which chapter is most appealing to you and your little ones and start there!

Do not feel rushed! Make sure to offer plenty of time to play with one setup before moving on to another one. We like to leave each setup for about a month. This gives your child plenty of time to go deeper with their play and has the added bonus of allowing you time to gather items needed for the next setup. Take your child's lead, watch them play, and see when you think they are ready to move on to a new scene.

Remember, play is supposed to be fun, so have fun with this book! Don't feel like what you create for your child has to look exactly like what is pictured here. These are ideas for you to take and make your own. We have time-savers suggested throughout the book for you and encourage you to use items you already have. Of course, if you enjoy crafting like we do, we have plenty of instructions for how to make the props we used so you can make them yourself too!

Throughout this book you will find callout boxes with some additional information:

Grown-Up Tip will have information to help you with the creation and setup of activities, and we offer time-saving advice or substitutions for you.

Let's Learn highlights the educational components of the activities, such as math, science, or language arts skills.

Age Adaptations offers suggestions for how to adjust the activities for older or younger children.

Skill Shout-Out points out the particular skills that your little one will be able to work on with each activity, such as fine or gross motor skills.

Extend the Play offers additional ideas for how to keep the fun going, using the materials you have already made in different ways.

What if your child doesn't want to play with these setups? We have all been there: you are excited about what you have created for your little one, you are sure they are going to love it, and they do—for two minutes—and then they walk away. What now?

reason we recommend leaving these activities set up for several weeks; having them available allows your child to continually pick their play back up and create deeper and richer scenarios over time.

Another way to encourage play is to draw on their interests. If your child has a show they love, pull in those characters and have those toys be the patients in the doctor's office. Or if they are very interested in writing, make sure to always include notepads and pencils in your setups. Or if they love cars, have them help you make a couple of cars out of boxes, including all their favorite elements, for the car wash instead of just you making one. You get the idea: if there is something your child is passionate about, include it in the play—that's part of the fun!

Think about their experiences. If your child has never been on a train, they may have a hard time imagining what it is like to take a train trip. That doesn't mean you can't make a pretend play train setup, but when you do your little one may need a bit more inspiration! Your local library is a great resource for situations like this. You can search their catalog or talk to the librarian and check out a few books on the topic to help get those creative juices flowing. For other setups, such as a coffee shop where you may go frequently, take a little time on your next trip to notice the details with your child and then remind them of what they saw when it is time to play.

Encourage them to consider all the people who may be a part of the situation. Help them think about who else might be in the place they are imagining. For example, an art gallery may have artists, visitors, curators, security guards, or even tour guides. This can help them take on a new role and put a whole new spin on the pretend play scene.

Keep in mind a child's attention span at their age. Generally speaking, your child's attention span will be about 2 to 3 minutes for every year, so if you have a five-year-old, you could expect them to stay focused on an activity for about 10 to 15 minutes. Of course, there is variation and factors such as interest, fatigue, or hunger, which can play a role as well, but being mindful of the average for your child's age can help you set your expectations. That is one

AVERAGE ATTENTION SPAN FOR AGES TWO TO SIX

2-year-old	4 to 6 minutes
3-year-old	6 to 9 minutes
4-year-old	8 to 12 minutes
5-year-old	10 to 15 minutes
6-year-old	12 to 18 minutes

WHAT IS PRETEND PLAY AND WHY IS IT IMPORTANT?

Pretend play is just what it sounds like: children pretend to be somewhere or someone they are not and play out those scenarios. They may pretend to be a teacher or imagine that they are on the moon. The play can be self-directed or an adult can set up a scenario for them to work from, but either way there are many benefits to be gained from this type of play.

One benefit is children can make sense of their world; they can rehearse things that may be new, exciting, anxiety-provoking, frightening, or intriguing and in that way develop a deeper understanding. Pretend play can also lead to a sense of control and mastery, which can be very comforting for young children who are working on learning so many skills.

Pretend play also has significant social and emotional benefits. Little ones practice taking on the perspectives of others, which can lead to empathy and a more thorough understanding of the point of view of others. They can also explore big emotions in a safe way. For example, we don't always encourage children to show frustration or jealousy, but when playing, all of those emotions are fair game.

Finally, pretend play is excellent for language development. When pretending, children have to be able to communicate what they are imagining so others can join in that world. Also, when taking on a new role or pretending to be in a new place, your little one will probably be using language that they may not use in their everyday life. For example, the space station may inspire talk about stars, planets, orbits, and experiments. Additionally, when children pretend to be adults, it tends to change the language they use as they try to imitate the adults they see around them.

SUPPLIES

Here are a few supplies we like to keep on hand:

- **Glue:** Hot glue, super glue, and glue sticks—we use them all.

- **Tape:** Masking tape, duct tape, and washi tape are our favorites. We love washi tape for decorating and on things we want to be able to remove easily (like from the floor!). Painter's tape is also good for that.

- **Foam board:** Lightweight yet sturdy and easy to decorate, it is a standby for all our projects.

- **Wooden crates:** Durable and flexible, wooden crates can be stacked to make a work surface, or use them as bins to hold supplies.

- **Cardboard boxes:** We like to save any sturdy cardboard boxes we come across, as they can be repurposed in so many ways!

- **Recyclable materials:** Empty paper towel and toilet paper tubes, jars, lids, plastic soap dispensers, and more are great ways to add props for play without needing to buy anything new.

- **Scissors:** A good pair of sharp scissors for adults and an age-appropriate pair for your child help immensely when crafting or doing activities. An X-Acto knife is also handy to keep around.

A note on sourcing supplies: We love to explore our local dollar stores for affordable supplies, and we have found great things in the automotive section for our pretend play car wash and the beauty section for our salon! Home improvement stores also have a surprising number of items you can repurpose for imaginative play; for example, we love to pick up river rocks in the garden section!

1

Detective Office

Time to hunt for clues! This month we are setting up a detective office for your little one to practice their skills of observation and deduction, or looking at a set of facts and coming to a logical conclusion. This is a skill they will need in order to make decisions for the rest of their lives and you can lay the foundations now. Your child can work at their desk or take their briefcase out in the field to gather clues and interview suspects. Playing detective is a great way to work on noticing details and also offers opportunities for your child to expand their vocabulary as they describe things in new ways. Your little detective can also gain confidence in their problem-solving skills as they create and solve their own mysteries.

TOOLS FOR PLAY

- Assorted office supplies, such as file folders, pens/pencils, notebooks
- Tape
- Kraft paper
- Black marker
- Magnifying glass
- Cardboard box the shape of a briefcase (approximately 12 × 9 × 4 inches [30 × 23 × 10 cm])
- Scissors
- Glue
- Extra cardboard scraps
- Yarn
- Photo of your child
- Construction paper
- White crayon
- White paper
- Watercolors and paintbrushes
- Ink pad
- Photographs (print at home or use an instant print camera!)

SETTING *the* SCENE

DETECTIVE OFFICE

Your detective needs an office to work in and a bulletin board to display the clues they find!

- Create a desk area with a small table. Add assorted office supplies, such as pens, notebooks, ink pads, and file folders.

- Tape a large piece of brown kraft paper to the wall and add a border with thick black marker. This will be your bulletin board where your little one can save all their clues and notes. You can do the same process with kraft paper to create a pretend office door!

- Add a magnifying glass to help them focus on details.

Grown-Up Tip: Washi tape or painter's tape will be easy for your child to use to add and remove notes from the bulletin board. Sticky notes also work well!

MAKE YOUR OWN PRETEND BRIEFCASE AND BADGE

BRIEFCASE

Every detective needs a way to carry their tools when they are on the job, and this briefcase fits the bill perfectly and is just the right size. You can also use an old briefcase you have on hand, but we like taking the opportunity to model getting creative with cardboard boxes. When your child sees all the different ways you can use a plain cardboard box, it can help them see the possibilities of what they themselves can create with a few simple supplies. It can be especially impactful if you involve them in the crafting process. Of course, time is not always on your side, so we definitely believe you should find a balance that works for you by having a combination of using real objects, crafting your own, and having your child help you craft them.

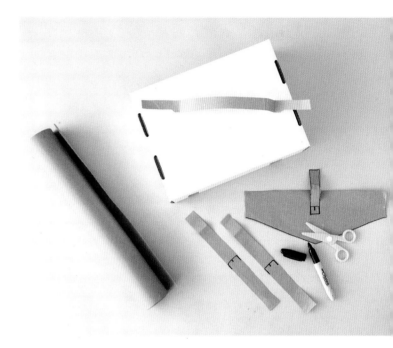

1. Place the cardboard box on your workspace.

2. Cut two 1-inch (5 cm) strips of kraft paper to wrap around the box as straps.

3. Cut a piece of kraft paper for the flap of the briefcase; it should be a rectangle the same length as the top of the box, with a triangular edge. Glue that to the front of the box. Take a smaller rectangle of kraft paper and glue it on as the buckle. Use a black marker to add stitching and buckle details.

4. Take a strip of thinner cardboard, like from a cereal box, and create the handle on the top of the box. Use glue to secure the ends down but leave the center free so your little one can hold the arch in the center.

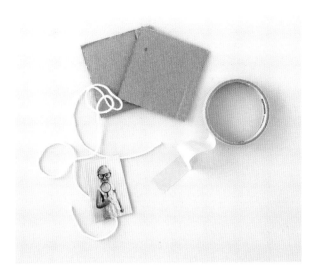

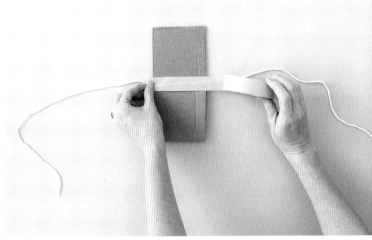

BADGE

Badges are a fun way for little ones to start learning how to write their names, and this one has the added fun of being able to flip open and closed. Just seeing their name written in different ways, such as all capital letters or with their first and last name, can really help your child prepare for when they need to be able to identify their name, for example when looking for their cubby/locker at daycare or school.

1. Cut two 4 × 4½-inch (10 × 11.5 cm) rectangles of cardboard. Take a piece of yarn, long enough to make a necklace, and tie the ends together.

2. Tape the cardboard rectangles together along their short ends, taping the yarn along that seam as well. This will make the "hinge" on the badge so it can be flipped open to show the inside. The yarn will allow your child to wear the badge around their neck.

3. Place a photo of your child inside the badge, and decorate the outside with a shield cut out of construction paper. You can also let your child decorate the badge.

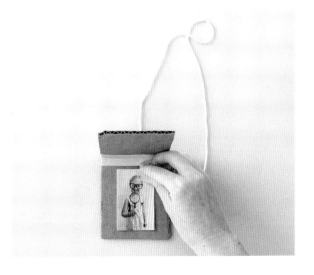

FINGERPRINTING ACTIVITY

Fingerprint activities are a simple way to dive right into noticing small details, from the different size prints fingers make to the whorls and patterns within each print! This activity is also very easy to set up; all you need is a piece of cardstock and an ink pad. You can add a magnifying glass if you would like to help encourage noticing details, but it works just as well without.

1. Create a grid for your little one to practice their numbers with fingerprints. A half sheet of cardstock is a great, sturdy option for this activity. Write numbers along the top of the sheet. For younger children, you can write them in order; for older children, you can mix it up. Using a marker, divide the card into sections so each number has its own column.

2. Give your child an ink pad and have them make the corresponding number of fingerprints in each column.

   Math skills: Your little one can work on their one to one correspondence with this activity, saying one number for each print they make.

Extend the Play: You can also use different color ink pads to make fingerprint patterns. Or even get two sets of fingerprints from the whole family and see if your little one can match them.

TAKE A SCAVENGER HUNT

A scavenger hunt is a fun way to practice following simple directions. You can also work on sequencing by asking your child to place the pictures of the clues in the order they found them. Sequencing is an important skill to practice. It will help your child make sense of words when learning to read, listening to stories, and even completing daily tasks.

1. Take photos of items that are around your child's play area and print them.

2. Create a trail for them to follow to find the photos. Give them the first photo clue and then when they go find that object, the second photo clue will be there. They then continue on the trail and find the next object in the photo.

3. You can hide a prize or a snack at the end of the hunt!

CREATE INVISIBLE INK MESSAGES

Hiding messages is a fun and playful way to work on early literacy skills. Little ones can focus on the shapes of the lines while older children can do more in-depth identification of letters, numbers, and shapes. This is also a wonderful opportunity to practice language that will help them when learning letter and number formation, such as talking about long and short lines, curving lines, and slanted lines.

1. Use a white crayon to draw secret messages on white paper. You can create these messages for your child to discover, or they can create them themselves. Maps and pictures of clues are fun for little ones to discover.

2. Uncover the messages by painting the paper with watercolors.

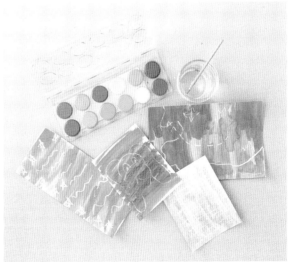

2

PRETEND PLAY

Post Office

Time to deliver some mail! This month we are setting up a post office where your little one can take on the role of postmaster by sorting and delivering all the mail. A post office is a great way to encourage early literacy in a low-pressure way. For little ones who are interested, writing their own letters can be incorporated, but for those who are not, the adult adding letters or simple words to the envelopes increases exposure to those concepts, which is still beneficial. This setup also provides plenty of opportunities to work on fine motor and math skills. Folding, stamping, and sealing letters help work those small muscles in the hands. The packing peanut sensory bin offers even more fine motor opportunities. Sorting helps little ones understand patterns, notice relationships between items, and identify sets, all of which lay a foundation for more complex mathematical thinking.

TOOLS FOR PLAY

- Copy paper box
- Markers
- Scissors
- Glue
- Poster board
- Wooden crates
- Bins
- Small boxes
- Kraft paper
- Envelopes
- Adhesive labels

- Bubble wrap
- Tissue box
- Paint and paintbrush
- Felt
- Yarn or ribbon
- Cardboard scraps
- Hole punch
- Packing peanuts
- Sponge
- Decorating items: pipe cleaners, googly eyes, etc.

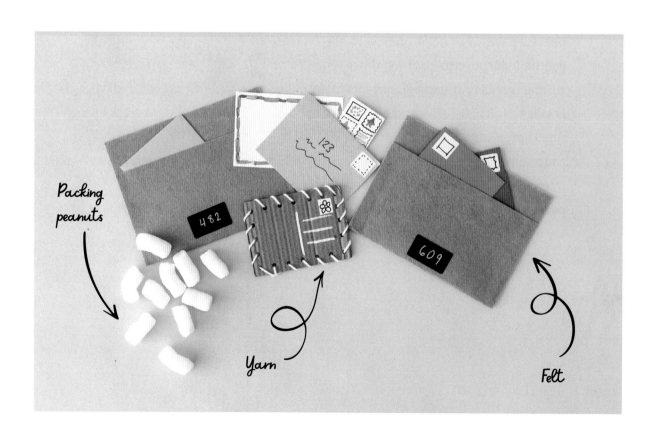

Packing peanuts

Yarn

Felt

Cardboard scraps

Small boxes

POST OFFICE

Your post office will need a place to collect the mail, sort the mail, and deliver the mail. You can make your own mailbox!

1. Take the lid of a copy paper box and stand it up on the short end. With markers, draw a rectangle toward the top half of the box: this will be your mail slot. Cut along three sides of your rectangle, leaving one of the long edges connected, and score along this edge to make your flap.

2. Carefully pull apart the top edge of the box, unsticking the flaps from the inside and straightening them so they stand upright on the outside of the top flap. Cut the small flaps so the edges are rounded; they should resemble half circles sticking above the body of the lid. Secure them in place with glue.

3. Glue a piece of poster board about 2 inches (5 cm) below the top edge of the box, then wrap it over the arched flaps you just made, securing with glue. This will make the curved top of your mailbox.

Grown-Up Tip: Save your boxes and the packing materials that come in them for this setup.

4. Create a counter for your postal worker to do their job by stacking wooden crates. The crates are especially helpful because they create shelves where you can store the materials needed.

5. Add bins for sorting, boxes wrapped in brown kraft paper, envelopes, adhesive labels, and bubble wrap as props for your little one to use.

CREATE A MAIL CARRIER AND MAILBOX

MAKE A MAIL CARRIER

Every postal worker needs a place to put the mail they collect on their rounds! Make your own out of a tissue box. While it seems like a simple activity, slipping letters into the box is great for working those motor skills, especially for younger children. The fact that the box is on a strap they are holding and not sitting still on a table makes it a little trickier!

1. Take a small tissue box, the kind with the rectangular opening in the center of the top. Remove the tissues and save for another use. Paint the tissue box.

2. Cut two narrow strips of felt and glue on either side of the opening. Glue two squares of felt on each of the strips to look like buckles.

3. Glue yarn or a ribbon to the sides to be your handle.

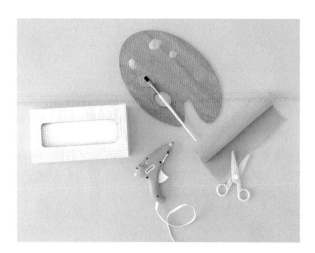

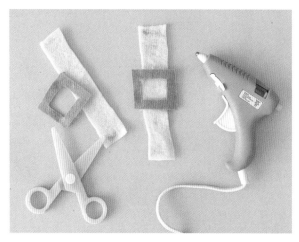

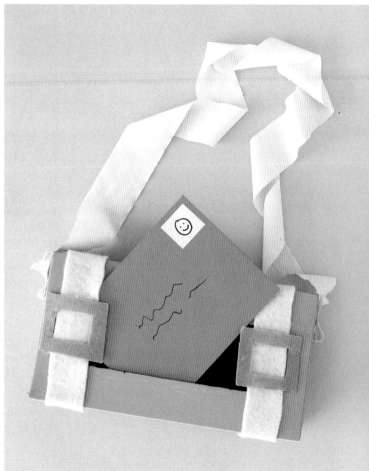

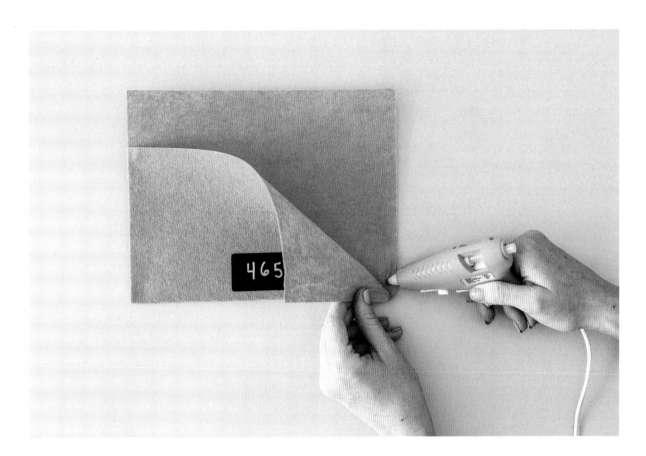

MAKE A WALL OF PO BOXES

For delivering mail, you can make a wall of
PO boxes with boxes so your mail carrier
has plenty of places to drop off those letters
and packages.

1. Take a sheet of stiff felt, put hot glue
along the long edges and fold the bottom
up approximately three-quarters of the
way to make a pocket. Use black labels,
or rectangles of paper, and glue or stick
to the front of the pocket.

2. Repeat the process until you have as
many boxes as desired.

3. Use reusable adhesive or tape to stick
them to the wall.

Grown-Up Tip: You can save time by
using hanging wall file organizers as your
PO boxes.

LETTER-SORTING ACTIVITY

Sorting is an important skill for your little one to develop, as it helps set the stage for later problem solving and also allows them to have a sense of mastery and control over their environment. Sorting letters is a fun way to work on this skill. Depending on where you hang your PO boxes, your little one can also get their body moving, reaching, bending, or walking from one area of PO boxes to another. Finding small ways to include gross motor skills in imaginative play setups helps the play last longer, so make sure you offer a large enough area for your child to play in.

1. Use the PO box wall and envelopes for this activity.

2. Label your PO boxes however you wish, with numbers, letters, or names. Whatever you choose, write those same things on a variety of envelopes.

3. Give the envelopes to your child and have them sort them into the proper mailboxes.

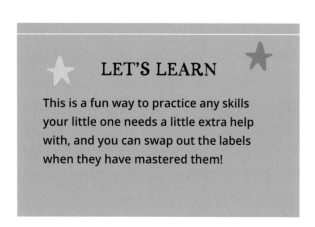

★ LET'S LEARN ★

This is a fun way to practice any skills your little one needs a little extra help with, and you can swap out the labels when they have mastered them!

FINE MOTOR STAMPS AND STICKERS

Creating your own stamps adds another layer of interest to a simple activity. Also, when children help create the props for their imaginative play setups, they tend to become even more invested in their play, and creating stamps is one of the easier ways to do that in this setup.

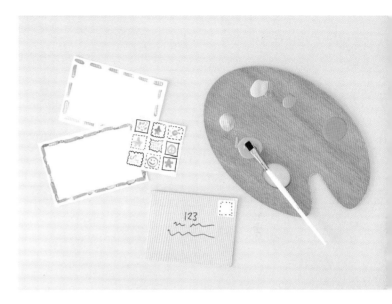

1. Use a black marker to draw three squares on each adhesive label. Cut them apart; you can cut down the entire sheet to make strips of stamps rather than cutting each label individually.

2. Let your child decorate them with markers.

3. You can also give them larger labels to decorate to make labels such as "Fragile," "Priority Mail," or "Overnight."

4. Let your little one use the stamps as they play, adding them to envelopes and packages.

SKILL SHOUT-OUT

Peeling and placing stickers is great fine motor practice and having different size stickers adds an extra element to the activity! Managing the larger labels requires more focus and skill so that they don't get folded in on themselves along the way.

MAKE YOUR OWN POSTCARD

These postcards can be used in multiple ways, not only for lacing and decorating. Once they are complete, your little one can use them in all areas of their post office, carrying them in their mail bag, sorting them into the post office boxes, and even sending them through the actual post office to friends and family. Making a real-world connection with their imaginative play always offers even more inspiration; if possible, heading to your local post office, purchasing a stamp, and placing the postcards in the box there is a wonderful opportunity for your child to see how their imaginative post office compares to a real one.

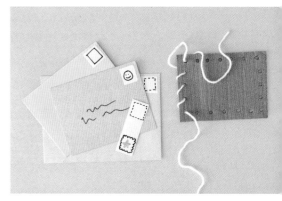

1. Cut a 4 × 6-inch (10 × 15 cm) piece of cardboard. Use a hole punch to punch holes all around the edges of the cardboard.

2. Using a marker, add the vertical line down the center of the postcard and horizontal lines on the right-hand side.

3. Tie a piece of yarn to one of the holes in the postcard and wrap the other end with a bit of tape to keep the end from fraying, or use shoelaces as the threading yarn.

4. Let your child thread the yarn through the holes.

5. They can also decorate the front of the postcard using paint, markers, stickers, etc.

Age Adaptations: For children who are writing, placing an address book in your post office is a wonderful addition to inspire them. You can use a small notebook with a few important addresses of family and friends, write them on index cards, or even list them on a sheet of paper you tape to the wall.

PACKING PEANUT CREATIONS

Exploring new textures is wonderful for children, and these packing peanuts become very different when damp, which also allows little ones to explore cause and effect. A material like packing peanuts that can be used in multiple ways is a fantastic way to add interest to an imaginative play setup and inspire creativity. Your little one is probably familiar with packing peanuts in boxes, but also showing them how to make sculptures with them can get those little wheels turning. You may be surprised with what else they can come up with!

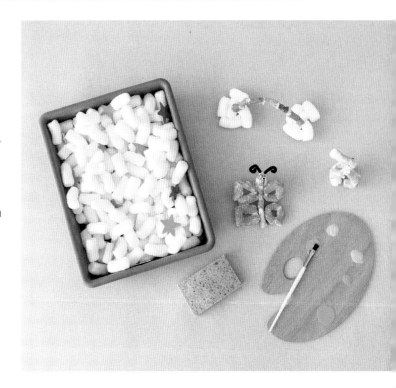

1. Fill a bin with biodegradable packing peanuts.

2. Wet a sponge, squeeze out most of the water, and set it next to the sensory bin.

3. Show your child how to make sculptures by gently dabbing the packing peanuts on the sponge to dampen them and then sticking them together.

4. You can use acrylic paint, googly eyes, pipe cleaners, and ribbon to decorate the sculptures once complete. Avoid any paint that is too watery or it will cause the sculptures to disintegrate.

 Grown-Up Tip: Let your child explore with just the packing peanuts before adding the sponge.

3

PRETEND PLAY

Spaceship

Let's set up a space station to inspire some out-of-this-world play! Setting up situations that are familiar to your child, such as a doctor's office, can be very valuable and is a great way to introduce this kind of imaginative play area, but you don't have to limit yourself to things your child has had hands-on experience with, as you can see with our space station. Exploring something new can allow your little one to make connections to what they already know and inspire questions to investigate. What better place to investigate than a space station? They can head to their very own command center and direct missions to the moon, where they can gather samples to explore. Watch your child take on the role of a scientist in outer space, which incorporates scientific thinking, language skills, math skills, and more.

TOOLS FOR PLAY

- 9 poster boards 22 × 28 inches (56 × 71 cm)
- Silver duct tape
- Foam board
- Scissors
- Construction paper
- Glue
- Paint and paintbrush
- Tri-fold presentation board 36 × 48 inches (91 × 122 cm)
- Fidget spinner
- Small chalkboard
- Calculator
- Outdoor thermometer
- Zipper
- Tap lights
- Recycled jar lids
- Keyboard
- Tinfoil
- Metallic paints
- Biodegradable glitter
- Rocks
- Toothbrush
- Mod Podge
- Cornstarch
- Food coloring

SPACESHIP

Make a spaceship for your little astronaut to use! This freestanding spaceship may seem difficult to construct, but really you are just making a tube out of posterboard and adding some embellishments. It is a simple project with a huge payoff. Having a spaceship as big as your child gives them a tangible base to work with, which is particularly helpful with a setup that relies so heavily on imagination. The closest your child has been to a real space station is most likely seeing exhibits in a museum. It also makes a statement, that their play is important and deserves to take up space in your lives.

1. Take six standard poster boards and lay them out on the floor in a large rectangle, three poster boards by two poster boards. Tape along the seams with silver duct tape. Roll into a large tube and tape together.

2. Add fins to the bottom by taping triangles of foam board on either side of your large tube. Decorate with stars, either painted or cut out of paper and taped on.

3. Make a window with a piece of construction paper and glue to the front of the large tube.

4. Add a top using two pieces of poster board and duct tape. Create a cone shape and place it on the top.

5. Cut a door out of the back: you can cut a rectangle away and leave an opening, or leave one side of the rectangle attached so the door will open and shut. You can add a third fin if you need more stability once the door is in use.

MAKE YOUR OWN COMMAND CENTER

This command center is a fun way to reuse old items. We have listed what we used here, but feel free to take a look around your house and see what you can find that will work. Look for things with buttons or moving parts for added fun. Home improvement stores and dollar stores are great sources for items to add to your command center as well!

1. Take a tri-fold presentation board and fold the side flaps back so that it stands on a small table.

2. Create your command center on the middle section of the presentation board. We used hot glue to add a fidget spinner, a small chalkboard, a calculator, a thermometer, a zipper, and tap lights. Add simple shapes made out of foam board for buttons and warnings, lids of jars for pretend knobs, and a foam board frame with space for a picture or map in the center. Use paint or paint pens to add hatch marks, numbers, and symbols as desired to turn these into buttons, knobs, and controls.

3. Place an old keyboard on the table in front of the presentation board.

CREATE A FOIL-STAMPED MOON

Heading outside at night to take a look at the moon can offer inspiration for this project as well as spark additional interest in this space setup. Looking up satellite images of the moon can also be a fun activity to prepare for making the moon.

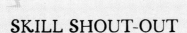

SKILL SHOUT-OUT

Squeezing the tinfoil is great fine motor practice!

1. Cut a large circle out of the posterboard.

2. Take large squares of tinfoil and have your children squeeze them into balls. These will be your painting tools!

3. Place several shades of metallic paint, such as silver, gold, and gray, on paper plates. Have your child dip the foil balls into the paint and stamp it on the posterboard to create the moon.

4. You can add glitter once the moon is dry to make it shine even more.

DECORATE MOON ROCKS

Painting rocks is an easy way to add depth and richness to your imaginative play setup: you can add them to a sensory bin, set them out with blocks or Magna-Tiles for building fun, or pile them around your spaceship so your child can incorporate them into their play.

1. Clean your rocks; you can purchase river rocks from a home improvement store or use rocks you find outside.

2. Use old toothbrushes and blue and white paint to splatter the paint onto the rocks.

3. Add biodegradable glitter and seal with Mod Podge.

Grown-Up Tip: This one can get messy, so paint the rocks outside, or place a large box on its side, place the rocks inside, and use that as your workspace.

HAVE FUN WITH GALAXY OOBLECK

Exploring different textures is very beneficial for your child. Each material you place in a sensory bin allows your little one to expand their range of what they are comfortable with. It is also a great way to work on fine motor skills and explore cause and effect.

1. Make a mixture of cornstarch and water using 1 part water to 1.5 parts cornstarch, adding purple food coloring to the water. Repeat the process and make a second batch but add black food coloring to the water.

2. Pour the two mixtures into a shallow bin, pouring each color in a separate area of the bin so the colors mix slowly but you can still see each individual color. Top with biodegradable glitter.

3. Let your little one explore!

Grown-Up Tip: When you are finished with this one, avoid putting it down the drain.

Extend the Play: This gooey mixture is fun to play with on its own, but adding a few simple items can engage your child longer. Try adding small figurines, spoons, scoops, or cups. Another way to change this activity up is to freeze the oobleck in ice cube trays or disposable cups.

4

PRETEND PLAY

Coffee Shop

Can you smell the coffee? In this coffee shop you can! In this chapter we are going to show you how to set up a coffee shop, complete with a scent-based sensory bin to really engage all the senses of your little one. Multisensory play is highly enriching, and incorporating scents into imaginative play is a unique way for your child to make connections with their previous experiences. While any type of shop lends itself to exploring with money and all the math skills associated with that, this shop has so much more. Your child will be able to fill coffee orders, sell treats, and even try their hand at designing their own packaging for coffee beans. The creative elements combined with the more concrete math aspects of the coffee shop will appeal to children with different interests and give them each an entry point to play. The coffee shop also provides a chance for your little one to mimic actions they see adults do all the time; this is not only fun for them but taking on an adult role also encourages a richer use of language as they copy your actions and how you speak.

TOOLS FOR PLAY

- Wooden crates
- Paper cups
- Napkins
- Coffee stir sticks
- Coffee pot
- Brown paper
- Milk carton
- Jars
- Pom-poms

- Cotton balls
- Black construction paper
- White paint pen
- Coffee beans
- Scoops
- Paper bags
- Cake stand or platters
- Washi tape
- Clear plastic bowls

- White plastic balls
- Yarn
- Index cards
- Decorating materials: paint, markers, stickers, crayons, etc.
- Cinnamon sticks
- Tea bags

Washi tape

Milk carton

Coffee pot

Paper cups

Max

Coffee stir sticks

Cotton balls

Brown paper

Napkins

Wooden crates

COFFEE SHOP

Create your bakery counter using wooden crates; stack them two by two and alternate which way they face so that they create shelves both behind and in front of the counter for your little one to use. Add items to the top of the counter to make your coffee bar.

- You can use real paper cups and lids, small napkins, coffee stir sticks, and even a coffee pot.

- Fill the coffee pot with crumpled brown paper.

- You can wash a real milk carton, let it dry, and paint it and include it in your coffee bar.

- Add small recycled jars with pom-poms and cotton balls for your sugar.

- Be sure to include a menu, which you can write on black construction paper with a white paint pen and use simple pictures or words to show what is available.

- Don't forget a tip jar!

- Add a large jar with coffee beans and a scoop along with brown paper bags so your little barista can sell bagged coffee.

- You can also create a section for baked goods, using a small cake stand or platters to display the treats.

- For a final touch, make a window on the wall with washi tape and make pendant lights to hang. Using lightweight plastic bowls, such as the ones you can find at a dollar store, hot glue a white plastic ball inside and tape a ribbon to the top to be the cord. Tape the lights to the ceiling.

MAKE PRETEND COFFEE SHOP TREATS

A cup of coffee pairs perfectly with a sweet treat! Having a few items that go together in a small shop is a great way to make sure the environment is rich enough to inspire play without getting too overwhelming.

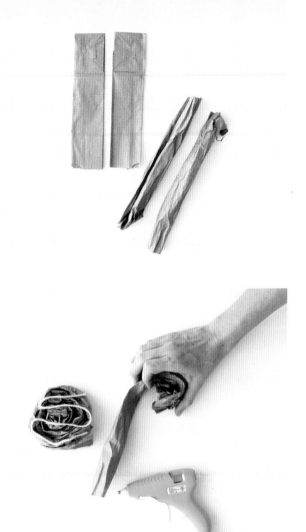

1. Cut a brown paper bag in half and roll it into a snake shape. Roll it into a cinnamon roll shape, securing with hot glue.

2. Glue pieces of yarn to the top to be the frosting. You can use basic white yarn for a vanilla frosting, or add different colors for different flavor rolls, such as brown for a chocolate roll and blue for a blueberry-flavored one.

3. Place on a cake stand or platter.

Extend the Play: Add items your child can use to serve up the treats, such as squares of wax paper to pick them up and small plates or bags to put them in.

DESIGN YOUR OWN COFFEE BAGS

Getting those artistic juices flowing by creating labels for the coffee bags adds another layer to this imaginative play setup. It can be helpful to have some quieter, more individual activities like this as well as ones that are more focused on interactions, both real and imaginary.

1. Use small brown paper bags and index cards to create bags of coffee beans for sale.

2. Set out index cards along with a variety of art supplies: you can use paint, markers, stickers, crayons, or anything else you have on hand for your child to use to decorate the cards. Once they are decorated, you can attach them to the front of the brown paper bags.

3. Your little one can then fill the bag up with real coffee beans, crumpled brown paper, or pom-poms so they are ready to sell to their customers!

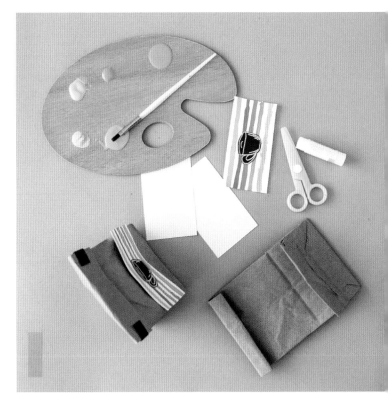

POM-POM COFFEE PLAY

Pom-poms are a fun stand-in for the various drinks found in a coffee shop, and for those who are ready, using the pom-poms as ingredients is a great way to practice following multi-step directions!

1. Fill several jars with pom-poms; you can use several shades of brown and tan as well as white to make different ingredients, such as milk, sugar, coffee, hot chocolate, and tea.

2. Add cardboard coffee cups, lids, and sleeves.

3. Fluffed cotton balls can stand in for whipped cream.

4. Let your little barista make their drinks by adding all the ingredients to the cups.

Age Adaptations: Younger children can have fun filling the cups with pom-poms; older children can use this activity to start exploring with volume, making small, medium, and large drinks. The oldest children can make and follow recipes to make different types of drinks, including different numbers and colors of pom-poms.

SENSORY JAR SMELL EXPERIENCE

We don't often think about engaging our sense of smell when playing, but it can really enrich the experience for young children, calling up memories and engaging them in a different way. A coffee shop is a logical place to start exploring scents, as there are such strong, easily identifiable ones that are associated with them!

1. Gather your scented items; whole coffee beans, cinnamon sticks, and tea bags are simple to use, but you can get as creative as you want. Just think about what scents you might come across at a coffee shop.

2. Place each item in a jar and let your child explore. They can try to identify the scents or recall a time they ate something including that ingredient.

Extend the Play: You can also put essential oils or extracts (such as vanilla) on cotton rounds and place those in the jars for your little one to identify for more of a challenge.

5

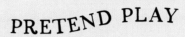

PRETEND PLAY

Art Museum

This chapter is all about letting your little one explore their artistic side! There are so many ways we can express ourselves, and in this art museum setup we have tried to offer a variety of avenues for your child to try out. For those who already have an affinity for creating in a certain way, such as drawing, they can incorporate that into their gallery. For those who are still exploring, they can try sculpture, mixed-media collages, even found object art! While some children are comfortable tackling new types of art projects, others can be a little more hesitant and having the structure provided by the art museum is helpful. They can curate an exhibit and create frames as well as make their own works of art. These projects are also fantastic fine motor practice. Talking about their art projects is also a fantastic language opportunity. Allowing your child to explain their thinking and describe what they did is a perfect example of working on metacognition, or understanding thought processes and the patterns underlying them. Try asking them to tell you about their art, what made them think to do it that way, and what they would name their artwork, or point out details that caught your eye. These can lead to much richer conversations than simply saying you like it and prompt that reflective thinking that is necessary for metacognition.

TOOLS FOR PLAY

- Wooden crates
- Fabric for draping
- Washi tape
- Black construction paper or chalk tape
- Ribbon
- Small stool or bench (optional)

- Assorted art supplies, such as paint, crayons, construction paper, air-dry clay, Styrofoam shapes, beads, etc.
- Easel
- Cardboard
- Glue

Beads

Fabric
for draping

Easel

Wooden crates

ART MUSEUM

There are two areas you can set up: the gallery space and the studio space. In the gallery area, stack boxes to create pedestals for sculptures, and drape the pedestals with fabric to cover the crates. On the walls, create frames with washi tape where the two-dimensional art can be displayed. Add small plaques made of black paper, or chalk tape, under where each piece of art is going to be displayed so you can add the artist's name, date, and title of their work. You can string up ribbon to keep visitors from touching the art and set out a small stool or bench so they can sit and enjoy the work. In the studio area you can arrange a variety of art supplies so your little one can make their creations to display in the gallery. You can stack crates and top with a small easel so that your artist can work standing up.

CURATE A COLLECTION AND CREATE YOUR OWN FRAMES

Every art museum needs exhibits, and this is a fun way to get the process started. Feel free to keep this simple or let your creativity run wild! If you feel like you need more material for your curator to sort through, a couple packs of postcards are an easy, affordable way to jump-start the process. It can be surprising what your child sees as a set. When they make their collection, try asking them what is the same about what they picked.

1. Talk to your child about creating a group of items that goes together, or curating a collection.

2. Let them to explore the house, create art, or take pictures of items that they feel belong in their collection. For example, if they want to create a collection about animals, maybe they will gather a picture of the family dog, make an animal figurine, and paint a picture of fish.

3. Have them display their collection in the art museum. They can hang things inside the frames you have created on the walls already, or make their own using washi tape. They can also embellish the frames using smaller pieces of washi tape if desired.

SKILL SHOUT-OUT

Creating a set is an important early math skill that your little one can practice with this activity!

SCULPT AN ARTIFACT CRAFT

Sculpture may be a bit more unfamiliar for your little one, but this simple project is a great entry point to creating three-dimensional art! Three-dimensional art is valuable for its own sake as a creative outlet but it also helps children with their spatial awareness.

1. Gather a variety of Styrofoam shapes, either saved from packages or purchased from a craft supply store or dollar store. Set them out with paint, pipe cleaners, and beads and allow your child to create their own sculpture.

2. If your little one needs a little more prompting, you can encourage them to paint the Styrofoam. While that is drying, they can begin threading beads on the pipe cleaners. Be sure to use beads that are an appropriate size for your child: younger children can use very large beads on thicker pipe cleaners while older ones can use smaller beads, such as pony beads. Once they have those components completed, they can combine them, sticking the pipe cleaners into the Styrofoam, bending and twisting it until they get the shape or design they like.

3. Once the sculpture is finished, glue it to a cardboard base and display it in the art gallery! Do not forget to fill out the plaque with the artist's information!

CREATE MONOCHROMATIC ARTWORK

Monochromatic art is often very striking; it is also a fabulous way to use up odds and ends of craft supplies. If you designate a bin for scraps while crafting, it makes it very easy to pull items for projects like this. Your child can also help sort items by color to help prepare.

1. Cut out a base shape from cardboard; it can be large or small and whatever shape your child desires.

2. You can even set out paint, chalk, or crayons in that color for your little one to use on the cardboard.

3. Set out a variety of materials all in the same color for your little one to create a collage on the cardboard base.

4. Use glue to secure the items on the base.

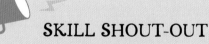

SKILL SHOUT-OUT

Exploring different shades of the same color, such as by describing them or naming them, is a great way to work on language skills.

Age Adaptations: Older children can mix their own shades of paint for this activity; just set out the base color along with white and black paint and a plate or some small cups for them to use as their palette.

6

PRETEND PLAY

Laundry Time

Time to do some laundry! In this chapter, we are going to help you set up a laundry station for your little one to play with. While laundry may seem like a never-ending chore to adults, for children the sensory component of laundry can be very enjoyable as well as the feeling of taking on a grown-up responsibility. Contributing to the household can be very rewarding for children, but in the day-to-day chore routine there isn't always enough time for them to master the necessary skills, which is why dramatic play setups like this laundry center are wonderful. Your little one can sort clothes, hang them up to dry, fold them, and more. They will be strengthening their fine motor skills, identifying colors, grouping items by attributes, and mastering practical life skills.

TOOLS FOR PLAY

- Cardboard box or poster board
- Scissors
- Cardboard
- Glue
- Tape
- Empty bottles
- Cotton fluff
- Jar
- Empty dryer sheet box
- White felt

- Yarn
- Handled scrub brush
- Tinfoil
- 4 laundry baskets/bin/boxes
- Index cards
- Clothespins
- Paint or markers
- Plastic bin
- Dish soap

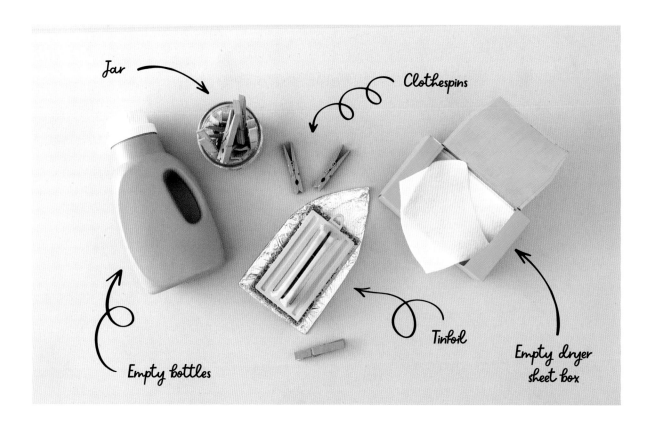

Empty bottles

Plastic bin

Cotton fluff

LAUNDRY TIME

Make your washing machine so your little one has a place to put all the dirty clothes.

1. Take a large cardboard box or a piece of poster board. Carefully cut a large circle out of the center, leaving approximately one-fourth of the circle attached on one side, making a door that will open and shut.

2. Cut circles of cardboard and glue them above the door to be your controls, or simply draw them on.

3. If you have used a poster board, you can tape it to the wall, and your child will be able to open and close the door. However, if you prop it up against something like a stool, they will still be able to place clothes "inside" the washer.

4. Add empty bottles to be used as the detergent. You can add cotton fluff to a jar as well to be your soap suds. Use an empty dryer sheet box and fill it with squares of white felt for your dryer sheets.

5. Hang up a piece of yarn to use as a clothesline. If you have a sturdy drying rack, you can set that out as well.

MAKE A PRETEND IRON

Using the real items, like recycled laundry detergent bottles, is not only fun, but makes setup easy. However, for something like an iron, where it is not so practical to use the real thing, this simple stand-in made out of cardboard and a sponge can still offer plenty of opportunities for fun!

1. Cut out a piece of cardboard to be the face of the iron; it should be roughly triangular and a little wider than the handled scrub brush.

2. Cover the cardboard with tinfoil and glue in place.

3. Paint the handled scrub brush if desired, and let dry.

4. Glue the scrub brush onto the center of the back of the iron to be the handle.

SOAPSUDS SENSORY BIN

Blending soap creates very dramatic, fluffy suds that make for a very engaging sensory bin!

1. Pour water into a sensory bin, enough to cover the bottom.

2. To make your soapsuds, place water and dish soap in a blender, approximately 2 tablespoons (30 ml) of soap for every ½ cup (120 ml) of water. Blend until very foamy.

3. Pour the suds into the sensory bin and let your little one play.

Extend the Play: Add a variety of sponges, small cups for scooping, and a second bin and let your child transfer suds from one bin to the other. Add doll clothes to the bin for washing.

LAUNDRY COLOR SORT

A laundromat is nothing without some laundry to wash, and this sorting activity offers a great way to incorporate all that laundry. Sorting is an important math skill where your child needs to identify objects, determine what is the same or different about them, and assign them to the proper category based on the guidelines set out. That is a lot of information to have to work with at one time! This activity allows you to customize the categories based on what laundry you have available as well as the sorting skills your little one has.

1. Set out four bins, boxes, laundry baskets, or plastic tubs.

2. Give your child assorted clothing items and have them sort them into the bins; they can sort by color, lights and darks, tops and bottoms, kid clothes and adult clothes, etc.

3. You can draw the categories on index cards and place them in the bins to help your child sort. For example, draw a shirt on a card for the shirt bin, or a red square on a card for the bin for red clothes.

Age Adaptations: Sorting is an important math skill; younger children can look at very simple categories, but older children can work with increasingly complex categories such as light tops, where they need to consider multiple attributes.

PRACTICE LAUNDRY FOLDING

Folding laundry is a real-life skill that can be tricky for little hands, so this folding board is the perfect way to help make that task a little easier. Children can practice folding without getting overly frustrated the way they might without the support of the board.

1. To make a folding board, take a rectangle of cardboard and draw "H" in the center. Cut the H apart; you should have two tall skinny rectangles on each end and two wide narrow rectangles stacked in the center.

2. Tape the board back together so it hinges, placing the tape over the top of each cut you made.

3. Cut the tape for just the bottom sides of the H, so that the center flap folds up.

4. Show your child how to use the board: place a shirt on the center, folding the ends of the arms in if needed so everything fits on the board. Flip the long sides into the center first, and then flip the bottom up; you should end up with a perfectly folded shirt.

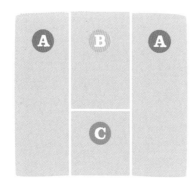
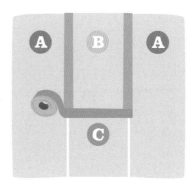

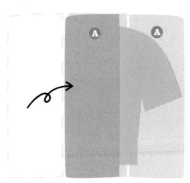
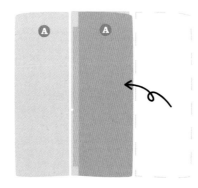
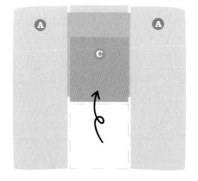
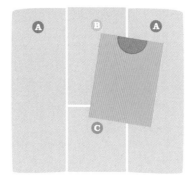

Extend the Play:
You can make a second folding board and have races to see who can fold their pile of shirts the fastest!

CLOTHESPIN MATCHING ACTIVITY

This simple activity allows children to work on identifying colors and is a great way to practice those fine motor skills!

1. Either paint your clothespins a variety of colors or purchase ones that are already colored.

2. Draw simple clothing items on index cards in the same colors at the clothespins. Or use real clothing items that are solid colors instead of drawing pictures on cards.

3. Have your child clip the cards to the clothesline with the corresponding color clip.

7

Ice Cream Shop

One scoop or two? This chapter is all about one of our favorite sweet treats: ice cream! Many kids love ice cream, but how often do they have the chance to scoop and serve it up themselves? This play setup gives them the chance to do just that. By combining real ice cream containers and scoops with pretend ice cream, your little one can play for hours without any fear of the ice cream melting. Another great element of a shop setup like this one is that it offers your child a chance to practice the real-life skill of ordering food. Your little one can take on the role of the customer and get more comfortable with speaking up for themselves and asking for what they want.

TOOLS FOR PLAY

- Poster board 22 × 28 inches (56 × 71 cm)
- Washi tape
- Painter's tape
- Cardboard boxes
- Thick yarn
- Toilet paper tubes
- Construction paper
- Tinfoil
- Hot glue
- Foam board
- Shaving cream
- Flour
- White glue
- Food coloring
- Foam paintbrush
- Acrylic paint
- Empty ice cream containers
- Tissue paper
- Ice cream scoop
- Cardstock
- Stapler
- Muffin tin

Ice cream scoop

Cardstock

Toilet paper tubes

Empty ice cream containers

Tissue paper

ICE CREAM SHOP

Define the space for your ice cream shop by making an awning, then add a big sign and a soft-serve machine and you will be ready to serve up some sweet treats!

AWNING

This awning is simple to make and can be used for a variety of other play setups.

1. On the piece of poster board, create stripes with strips of washi tape.

2. Fold the long edge of the poster board under, making a flap that is several inches wide. This is the side that you will tape to the wall. Fold the opposite edge under to make a thinner band. Tape the thick band to the wall with painter's tape and enjoy your awning.

SOFT-SERVE MACHINE

Most children have an ice cream scoop in their house for serving ice cream, but who has a soft-serve machine? Adding something new to something familiar is a great way to extend the play.

1. Start by making the body of your machine. You want the front of your box to be mostly open, with two tabs at the top to serve as your ice cream dispensers.

2. For your ice cream, you'll have two different colors of yarn to be your two flavors. Depending on the thickness of your yarn, take several strands that are about the length of your box and twist them gently together. Tape a twist to the top of your box behind each tab. Feed the bottom of the twist into a toilet paper tube and tape inside. The tube should sit comfortably on the bottom of the box. You can add a construction paper collar to the top of your toilet paper tube to make it look like a wafer cone.

3. Add a handle to the side of your machine. Take a strip of cardboard and wrap it with tinfoil. Glue the ends of the strip to the box to make a loop, leaving the top free.

4. Finally add your signs. Take a piece of cardboard and draw an ice cream cone on it, fold the bottom edge back so it stands up, and tape to the top of your machine, then label your dispensers with what the ice cream flavors are.

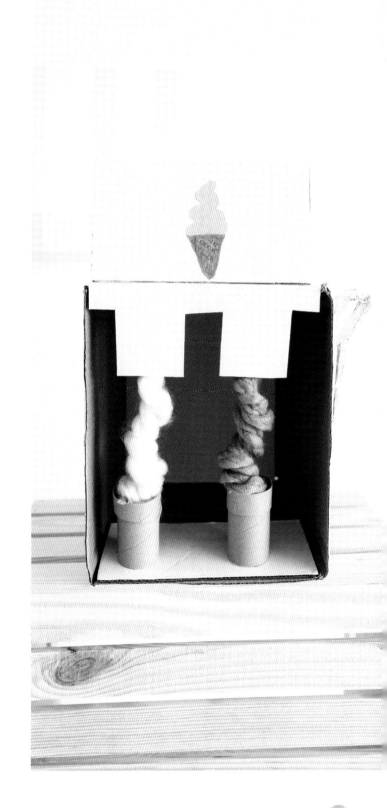

PUFFY PAINT ICE CREAM SIGN

A larger-than-life ice cream cone sets the tone for fun! Feel free to make your ice cream any color you like; simply swap out the pink food coloring for your desired color. We find, generally speaking, that gel food coloring makes for more vivid colors and the liquid creates more pastel tones.

1. Cut a large, basic ice cream cone shape out of your foam board.

2. Make puffy paint to use on the ice cream portion of the cone by mixing ¾ cup (40 g) shaving cream, ¼ cup (30 g) flour, ¼ cup (60 ml) white glue, and a few drops of pink food coloring.

3. Use the puffy paint to paint the ice cream scoop; layering it on thickly with a foam paintbrush works well!

4. Use brown acrylic paint to paint the cone portion of your sign. You can create the grid design while the paint is still wet by dragging the end of the paintbrush through it.

5. Let dry completely and then display: you can tape it directly to the wall, or tape it to a box to prop it up at the entrance to your ice cream shop.

MAKE YOUR OWN ICE CREAM

An ice cream shop needs ice cream! This ice cream won't melt and is easy for little ones to scoop up with a real ice cream scoop.

1. Eat some ice cream, then wash and dry the tubs.

2. Paint the outside of the tubs to match your flavors: pink for strawberry, brown for chocolate, white for vanilla, and green for mint chocolate chip.

3. Crumple coordinating colors of tissue paper to make balls; these will be your scoops of ice cream. Draw black dots on the green tissue paper before crumpling for the chocolate chips.

4. Put the ice cream in your containers and add a scoop!

LET'S LEARN

Sorting the ice cream into the proper containers will help your child as they establish an understanding of patterns and relationships. They are working on comparing different items to see how they are the same and different, and laying the foundation with a simple activity like this will help them as they begin to work with more complicated attribute rules and sets of items.

MAKE AN ICE CREAM SHOP HAT

Sometimes all it takes to get into character is a hat! Dressing the part can help younger children take on a new role and also serves as a reminder of who is who when playing with others.

1. Take two pieces of tissue paper and place them on top of each other. Accordion-fold them along the long edge, making each fold about 1 inch (2.5 cm) wide.

2. Cut a sheet of cardstock in half along the long end. Glue the long edge of the folded tissue paper onto the top edge of one of the pieces of cardstock. Repeat with the other piece of cardstock on the other side.

3. Place your two pieces of cardstock together, with the tissue paper sandwiched in the middle, and staple the short edges together.

4. Use paint or markers to decorate the outside of the ice cream hat.

5. You can then gently pull the center of the cardstock apart and place the open side on your child's head as a hat.

ICE CREAM SORTING ACTIVITY

When introducing a new imaginative play setup, offering an activity that allows your child to use the props with a purpose, such as sorting, helps them see the different ways they can use the items and inspires creativity moving forward.

1. Use the ice cream scooping supplies for this activity! Take circles of the same tissue paper you used to make the balls of ice cream and place them in the bottom of a muffin tin (you may need to layer several circles so the color is bright enough for your little one to see).

2. Have your child use the scoop and place the ice cream balls in the wells of the muffin tin, matching the colors.

 Extend the Play: Make a pattern in the top row of the muffin tin and have your little one copy it in the bottom row.

PRETEND PLAY WORKSHOP FOR KIDS

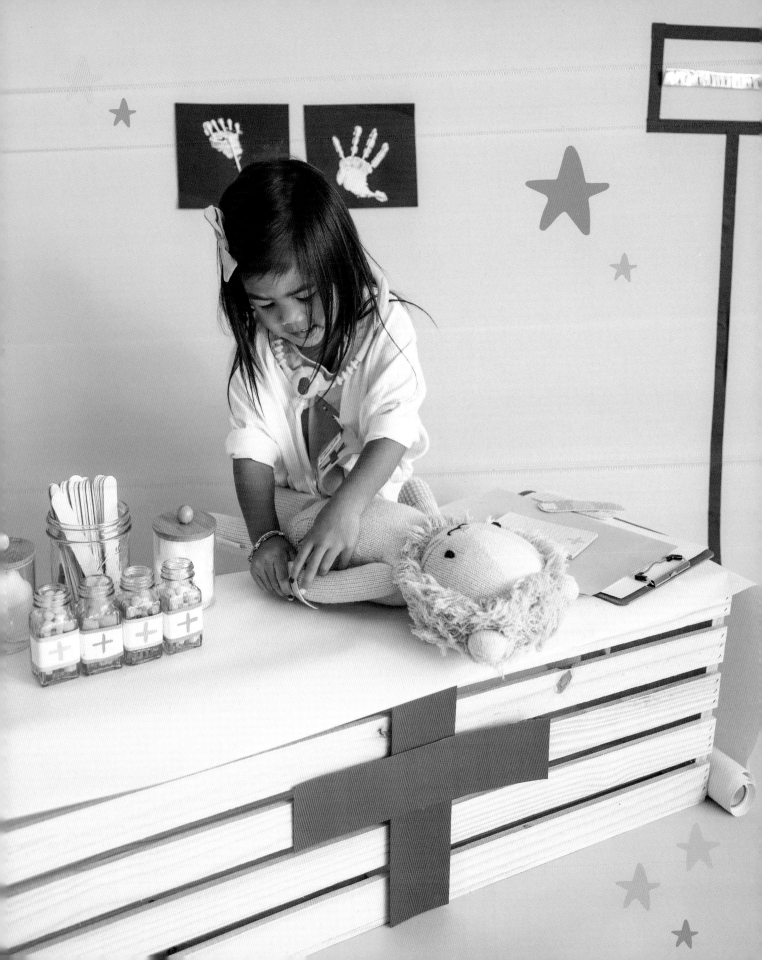

8

Doctor's Office

Time for a checkup! In this chapter we are creating a doctor's office where your little one can draw from their own experiences at the doctor to play and explore. We will show you how to set up a waiting room, an exam room, and even a pharmacy station so your little doctor can take care of all their patients' needs. This pretend play setup offers plenty of opportunities to explore mathematical concepts, as there are numbers, volumes, categories, and more, as well as scientific concepts, such as how the body works. There is also great potential for social and emotional learning as well; taking on the role of caring for others lets your little one practice empathy and taking the perspective of others. This doctor's office also allows your child to work through any nerves or fears they have about visiting the doctor themselves; with their own personal office, they control the situation and can role-play any elements they wish as often as they want.

TOOLS FOR PLAY

- Wooden crates
- Red paper
- Tape
- Clipboards
- File folders
- Pencils
- Cardboard
- Scissors
- Date stamp and ink pad (optional)
- Roll of white paper
- Black washi tape
- Markers
- White pen
- Small jars
- Popsicle sticks
- Cotton swabs
- Cotton balls
- Bandages
- Masks
- Gauze
- Small notepad
- White T-shirt
- Iron-on adhesive (optional)
- Felt
- Small photo of your child
- Badge clip
- Velcro
- White paint
- Black cardstock
- Yarn
- Clothespins
- Pom-poms
- Tongs (optional)
- Dot stickers
- Tube socks

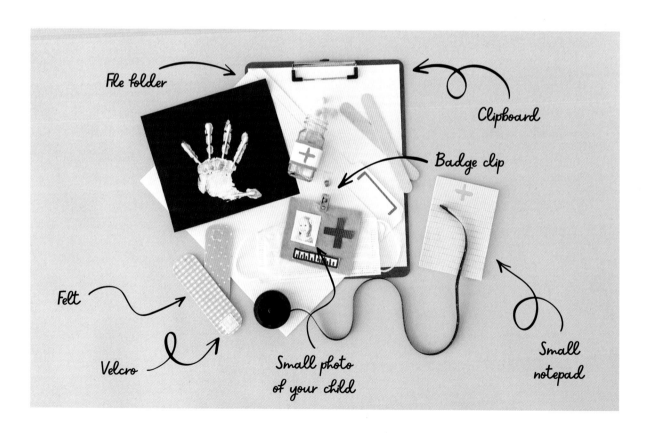

File folder

Clipboard

Badge clip

Felt

Velcro

Small photo of your child

Small notepad

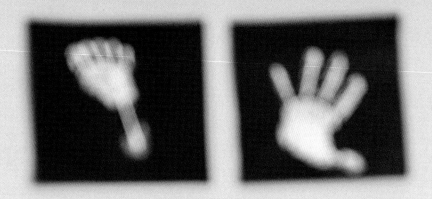

Popsicle sticks

Pom-poms

Small jars

Gauze

DOCTOR'S OFFICE

To make a doctor's office setup, you'll need a check-in area and an exam room.

CHECK-IN AREA

1. Create a desk out of stacked crates or boxes, and tape a red cross to the front with two strips of red paper.

2. Add clipboards, file folders, and pencils. You can make a play laptop with cardboard: fold a rectangle of cardboard in half, cut small squares of cardboard to be the keys, and glue them to the bottom half the larger piece, then cut a rectangle slightly smaller than the top half of the larger piece and glue it above the keys to be the screen. Paint the whole thing. You can glue ribbons to the sides of the laptop to help the screen stay open.

3. A date stamp and an ink pad are fun additions.

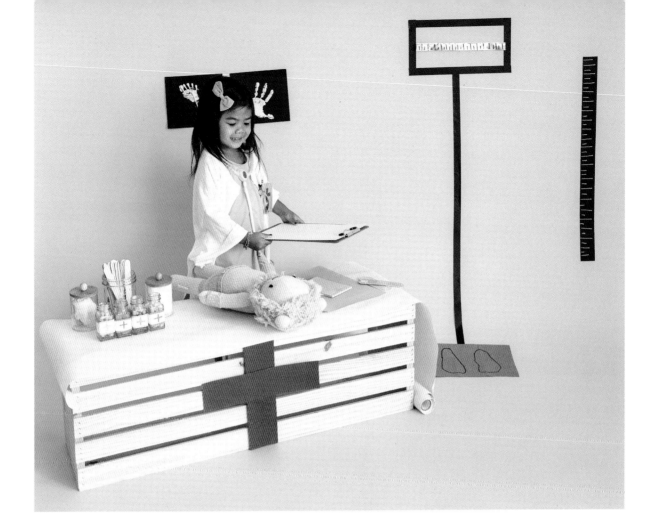

EXAM ROOM

1. Put two wooden crates next to each other and place white paper on top to make the exam table.

2. Use black washi tape to make a scale on the wall: use two long strips to make a column and top it with a rectangle of tape. Place a strip of silver tape across the middle of the rectangle and add hash marks with black permanent marker. Put a rectangle of cardboard on the floor at the base of the column with footprint outlines on it.

3. Use black washi tape to make a height chart on the wall, making hash marks with a white marker.

4. Add various medical items, such as jars with wide popsicle sticks, cotton swabs, cotton balls, bandages, masks, and rolls of gauze. If you already have a toy medical kit, you can add those items to the setup!

5. Add a small notepad and pencil for your little one to write prescriptions on.

MAKE YOUR OWN DOCTOR'S COAT AND BADGE

Looking the part is important, and a white coat and badge are key elements of a doctor's outfit! If you already have a dress-up set that includes a doctor's coat, feel free to use that; if not, you can make this simple one with an old T-shirt, glue, and felt.

DOCTOR'S COAT

1. Find an oversized large white T-shirt that can be cut. If you can't find one, you can always pick up a new one at the store.

2. Cut off the bottom of the T-shirt so that it is a good length for your child; save that fabric.

3. Cut down the center of the front, so the shirt opens like a jacket.

4. Use the scraps of fabric from the bottom to create pockets; either glue them on or use iron-on adhesive to secure.

5. Add strips of felt to the top edge of the pockets; this helps give them a little more structure and makes it easier for your child to use.

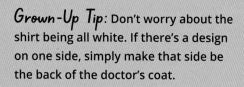
Grown-Up Tip: Don't worry about the shirt being all white. If there's a design on one side, simply make that side be the back of the doctor's coat.

DOCTOR'S BADGE

1. Cut a rectangle out of felt.

2. Print a small photo of your child's face.

3. Glue or tape it to the badge and add another strip of paper where you can write your child's name below it. You can also add what type of doctor they would like to be!

4. Cut a red cross out of felt and glue it to the badge next to your child's picture.

5. Put a badge clip on the top of the badge and attach it to the lab coat with a small piece of Velcro.

Age Adaptations: Older children can write on their own badges. Writing something that is meaningful to them and can be used in play can be very motivating!

X-RAY CRAFT

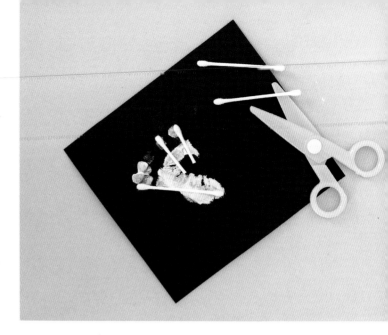

This project involves fine motor skills, but also allows your child to explore the human body in a new way, thinking about what makes our bodies work, mainly the structure of our skeletons.

1. Your little one can make X-rays to display in the office. Using white paint, paint your little one's hand or foot.

2. Press their painted hand or foot onto a piece of black construction paper to make an imprint.

3. Glue cotton swabs on the imprint as bones.

4. Make an area to display the X-rays by hanging a length of yarn or ribbon and adding clothespins. Your little one can easily pull down X-rays they would like to examine closer and hang them back up when they are done.

SKILL SHOUT-OUT

Using clothespins is great fine motor practice and doing it while standing up can be trickier than it seems for our youngest ones!

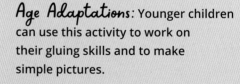

Age Adaptations: Younger children can use this activity to work on their gluing skills and to make simple pictures.

POM-POM PRESCRIPTION SORTING ACTIVITY

Sorting is a great way to recognize attributes. Comparing and contrasting different items develops language skills (you have to find ways to describe what is the same and different about the items). Sorting is also great help for developing math skills (working on one-to-one correspondence and seeing the relationship between objects).

 Take several jars and cut strips of paper to wrap around them as the labels. Draw crosses on the front with markers in the colors of your pom-poms. Or use paper cups instead of the jars, so you can write directly on them with markers. Younger children can have jars with single colors, while older children can sort multiple colors into the same jar.

 Set out pom-poms with the jars and have your child sort them. For extra fine motor practice they can use tongs to place the pom-poms in the jars.

FINE MOTOR BANDAGE ACTIVITY

Fine motor skills are incredibly important for children to develop. Strong fine motor skills are important for writing, but think about all the other tasks that require strong fingers, such as opening and closing containers, zipping a jacket, building with Legos and more.

1. Use a large piece of kraft paper to trace a stuffed animal.

2. Scatter dots throughout the interior of the body outline. You can do this, or have your child do it with dot stickers for extra fine motor practice.

3. Then, have your little one use bandages to cover up each of the dots.

SKILL SHOUT-OUT

This is a great way to include language about different body parts and also prepositions of place, such as "above," "below," "next to," and "between."

MAKE A PRETEND CAST

While we definitely encourage you to use a pretend play doctor's set, if you have one, there are a few items you can add to make this imaginative play setup extra special, and this cast is one of them. Adding a few new props can make all the difference when revisiting an old favorite.

1. Take a small tube sock and cut off the end, leaving just the part of the sock that would be above the ankle.

2. Your child can slide it over their arm as a cast. They can also decorate it with markers if desired.

3. To make a foot cast, just cut off the toes of a tube sock, leaving the heel, and your child can slip it on over their foot.

WEIGHT AND MEASURING ACTIVITY

Measuring and weighing allow children to work with numbers, from simple numeral recognition to working with attributes (more versus less); this lays a good foundation for future math skills.

1. Let your child use the height chart to measure the heights of their patients. Sticky notes are a fun addition to help them keep track of how tall each patient is.

2. Use a roll of white paper to cover the "exam table" and set out colored pencils or crayons for your little one to use to mark the length of their patients.

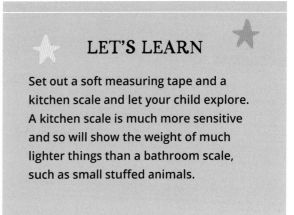

LET'S LEARN

Set out a soft measuring tape and a kitchen scale and let your child explore. A kitchen scale is much more sensitive and so will show the weight of much lighter things than a bathroom scale, such as small stuffed animals.

9

Hair Salon

Time to head to the salon! In this chapter we are going to show you how to set up a salon where your little one can care for all types of hair. They will be able to buzz, wash, and clip hair—pretend hair, that is! Yarn haircuts allow children to work with scissors in a fun and unique way, while the hair tie tower allows them to practice real-world skills and strengthen their fine motor skills. Those first haircuts can also be tricky for little ones, so, similar to the doctor's office, this salon allows children to work through some of the nerves they may have about going to get their own haircuts, or even struggles they have getting their hair done on a daily basis. While some may think of a salon as a more feminine imaginative play setup, we would like to challenge that idea. People of all genders get haircuts and we think it is important to offer opportunities for play that don't conform to gender stereotypes.

TOOLS FOR PLAY

- Wooden crates
- Assorted hair accessories, including rollers, combs, handheld mirrors, hair ties, bows, etc.
- Old shampoo bottles
- Small stools or chairs
- Tape
- Tinfoil
- Foam board
- Plastic tub

- Gold paper
- Paper towel tubes
- Scissors
- Vinyl tablecloths
- Paper cups
- Toilet paper tubes
- Glue
- Paint and markers
- Yarn
- Stapler

- Cardboard
- Velcro tape
- Construction paper
- Paper plates
- Child scissors
- Balloons
- Shaving cream
- Tongue depressors

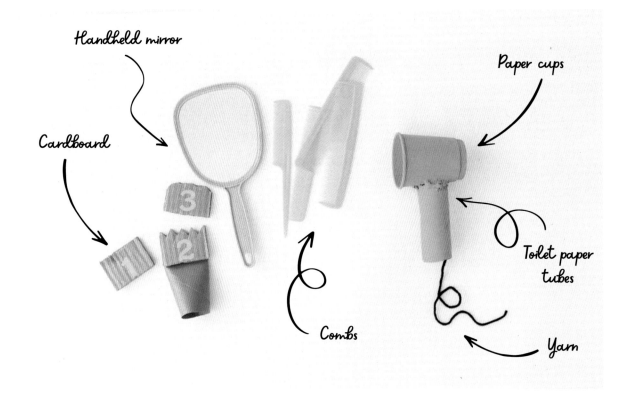

Handheld mirror

Cardboard

Paper cups

Combs

Toilet paper tubes

Yarn

Paper towel tubes

Gold paper

Construction paper

Vinyl tablecloths

Rollers

Small stools or chairs

Wooden crates

HAIR SALON

Create your salon stations.

- Use a crate for each station, placing it upright on the short end. Your hairdresser or barber can put their tools on top of or inside the crate, such as handheld mirrors, combs, plastic curlers, and old shampoo bottles.

- Put a small chair or stool in front of each crate for the customer to sit in. Add mirrors to each station by taping a large piece of tinfoil to a slightly larger piece of foam board. Tape each mirror above a crate.

- To make a hair washing station, simply place a plastic tub on top of one of the crates.

- Add a light above each station by wrapping a piece of gold paper around an empty paper towel tube and taping it in place. Tape this light to the wall above the mirror.

- To make capes for the salon customers, cut a simple poncho shape out of vinyl tablecloths. Cut a rectangle 20 inches (50 cm) across and 52 inches (132 cm) long and fold in half to make a 20 × 26-inch (50 × 66 cm) rectangle. On the center of the folded edge cut a half circle about 5½ inches (14 cm) wide to make the opening that will fit over their head.

PRETEND HAIR DRYER AND RAZOR CRAFT

Including a pretend hair dryer and razor in your salon allows children with a variety of hair types and styles to find the tools that they recognize from their visits to the salon.

HAIR DRYER

1. Take a paper cup and an empty toilet paper roll and cut the end of the roll if needed so it sits more flush against the side of the cup. Glue the tube to the side of the cup, positioning it on the smaller, bottom edge.

2. Use paint or markers to color it.

3. Tape or glue a piece of yarn to the inside of the tube to be the cord.

RAZOR

1. Take an empty toilet paper tube and staple one end closed.

2. Paint the tube whatever color you desire.

3. Make the various hair clipper guards to go on the razor by cutting rectangles out of cardboard; you can cut different patterns along the top of each rectangle. Add a number to each guard.

4. Attach Velcro dots to the closed end of the toilet paper tube and to the back of each guard so you can attach them and swap out the different sizes.

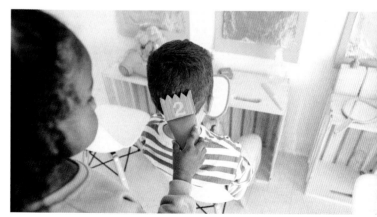

HAVE FUN WITH YARN HAIRCUTS

Some grown-ups may be intimidated by introducing a haircutting activity to young children; after all, we often spend time emphasizing NOT cutting hair. With this activity it can help to set very clear expectations, such as the scissors are for cutting the yarn only. Feel free to add clips, ribbons, and elastic bands for your child to use to complete the styles they create!

1. Paint several paper plates a variety of skin tone colors and let dry.

2. Cut out simple shapes to make eyes, noses, and mouths from construction paper and glue onto the plates.

3. Glue yarn to the plates to create the hair to cut. You can add different amounts to each plate for your child to work with as they style the hair.

4. Let your little one use child scissors to cut the yarn to make whatever hairstyles they desire. They can also add bows to accessorize their looks when they are done.

Grown-Up Tip: The thinner the yarn, the easier it will be for your child to cut, so save the thicker yarn for older children who have stronger scissor skills and can use sharper scissors!

BUILD A HAIR TIE TOWER

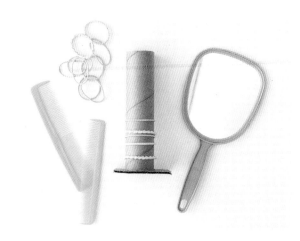

Letting your little one use hair ties is a unique way to work on fine motor skills, and also allows them to practice real-life skills.

1. Cut a square of cardboard and glue a paper towel tube to the center of it.

2. Set out the tower with a bowl of hair ties and have your little one stretch them out and put them on the tower.

LET'S LEARN

You can also use this activity to practice making patterns. Just get hair ties in a variety of colors to use!

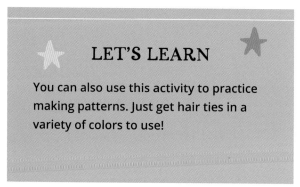

SHAVING CREAM PLAY

This is a great activity for those who may be a bit hesitant to explore sensory experiences that are messy. Using a tool like the tongue depressor and having water close by to rinse off when needed can offer just enough support so they are comfortable playing with shaving cream.

1. Blow up a balloon and add a face to the front with a marker.

2. Spread shaving cream on the balloon. Your little one can shave the top of the head, the beard, or both!

3. "Shave" the cream off with a large tongue depressor. Make sure you have a tub of water nearby for rinsing off the tongue depressor.

Grown-Up Tip: To help keep the balloon head from floating away, you can tape it to a dowel which can then be placed in a jar or stuck in a piece of Styrofoam.

10

Car Wash

Time to wash those cars! This car wash setup adds a new spin for littles who are interested in vehicles. Once cars are done driving you can still find ways to play with them. Your child can build their own car out of a cardboard box and then use that car in their car wash. There are many wonderful sensory and motor components this month, from moving all around the car to squeezing the sponges and exploring a car wash sensory bin; your little one will be on the move and taking in that sensory input, which is so important for moving through the world.

TOOLS FOR PLAY

- Pool noodles
- Tape
- Blue streamers
- Tulle
- String
- Paint and paintbrush
- Foam board
- Cardboard tubes
- Plastic cones

- Buckets
- Sponges
- Tool caddy
- Spray bottles
- Squeegees
- Cleaning cloths
- Boxes approximately 18 × 12 × 6 inches (45 × 30 × 15 cm)

- Glue
- Construction paper
- Ribbon
- Calculator
- Silver duct tape
- Wooden coins
- Washable paint

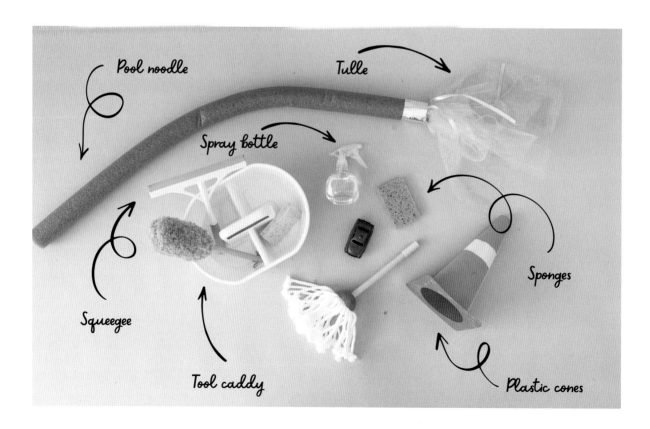

Blue streamers

Silver
duct tape

Calculator

Foam board

Tool caddy

Plastic cones

CAR WASH

To create your water wall, use a pool noodle and two rolls of blue streamers. Tape streamers all along the noodle. Once they are attached, roll the noodle a few times so the streamers wrap around it, covering the tape and making them a bit more secure. Attach four pieces of wide glitter tulle to the noodle. Tie string around the ends of the noodle and tape it to the ceiling. Make signs to instruct your little drivers what to do. Paint a stoplight on a piece of foam board and paint a simple car on another piece of foam board. You can create stands by gluing cardboard tubes to pieces of foam board/cardboard or use things you already have; we like using our wooden pretend play mop stand! Add plastic cones, buckets, sponges, a caddy, spray bottles, a squeegee, and cleaning cloths.

Grown-Up Tip: Check out the automotive section at a dollar store to find supplies!

MAKE A PRETEND CAR WITH A CARDBOARD BOX

A car is arguably one of the most important elements of a car wash, and this one has the added benefit of being able to be worn by your child! If a group is playing at the car wash, one child can wear the car and drive it through the setup while the others wash. If a child is playing solo, this car is still a fun prop that works well even without a child wearing it.

1. Fold all the bottom flaps up into the box and glue them in place; this adds support while leaving the bottom open.

2. Fold the flaps from the long sides on the top of the box in and glue them in place as well.

3. Take the shorter flap on the front of the car and leave it as is, creating a little shelf on the front of the car to hold the steering wheel. Glue in place.

4. Cut the shorter flap on the back of the car in half and glue in place, creating a shorter shelf on the back of the car.

5. Make the steering wheel by cutting a toilet paper tube in half and gluing a cardboard circle on top. Paint it black and allow it to dry. Glue a circle of white cardstock to the center of the circle and glue the entire thing to the front flap of the car.

Grown-Up Tip: If you don't have time to make this car, you can attach cardboard circles (for tires and a steering wheel) to a laundry basket for a faster option.

6. Make tires, headlights, and taillights out of circles of black and white cardstock and glue onto the body of the car.

7. Make shoulder straps out of ribbon, attaching them to the inside of the car with glue.

Extend the Play: These instructions make a simple car, but feel free to add more details. You can involve your child in the process and look at real cars to get inspiration for what else to include.

BUILD A PAY STATION

This is a fun way for your child to explore with money that is a little different than the traditional cash register. They can count the coins as they put them in the slot and afterward sort the coins that have come through. Coins are also a great way to practice skip counting; use nickels to work on counting by fives and dimes to practice counting by tens.

1. Glue an old calculator to the bottom of a box, paint the whole bottom, and let dry.

2. Add a coin slot. Cover a small piece of foam board with silver duct tape and glue to the box above the calculator. Cut a rectangle all the way through the foam and the bottom of the box so your child can slip coins through.

3. Prop the pay station on a wooden crate and add coins for your little one to use with it. We like sturdy Magic Playbook wooden coins for this activity, as they are a little larger and easier to slide through the slot for little fingers.

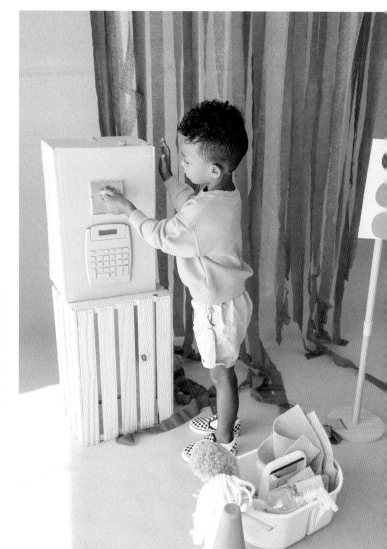

⭐ LET'S LEARN ⭐

Coins are a fun way to work with numbers, from counting to skip counting to simple addition and subtraction!

MAKE A CAR WASH HOSE

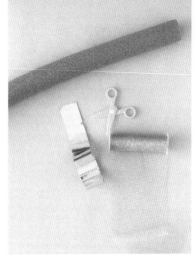

In order to wash a car, you need water, and that is where this hose comes in! Using a variety of ribbons and tulle really makes the "water" fun and is a great way to use up scraps you have on hand.

1. Take a pool noodle and attach ribbons and tulle to the end with silver duct tape; you can use glitter tulle, blue tulle, and blue ribbons.

2. Add an extra layer of duct tape to make sure everything is secure and there are no loose ends.

3. You can also cut down the noodle to make it shorter and more manageable for little hands.

SKILL SHOUT-OUT

Using this hose is a great way to incorporate gross motor skills into play. To really get your little one moving, you can make "dirt" for them to find and wash off the car; sticky notes are easy to place and remove.

SPONGE SQUEEZING TRANSFER ACTIVITY

Squeezing sponges can be engaging all on its own, but adding a few simple buckets and giving your child a task can really extend their interest in the activity as well as inspire more imaginative play scenarios. You can also offer a variety of types and sizes of sponges for this activity and your child can see which ones work best for moving water.

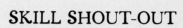

SKILL SHOUT-OUT

Squeezing sponges is great fine motor practice, and to add gross motor practice, spread the buckets out, or place them on different surfaces so your child has to stretch and reach during this activity.

1. Take various containers and wrap strips of washi tape around them at different heights to make fill lines.

2. Add a bucket of water and sponges and have your little one use the sponges to transfer the water, filling each container up to the fill line.

TOY CAR WASH SENSORY BIN

Sensory bins allow your child to explore different textures but also work on fine motor skills and real-life skills. This bin lets them work on using spray bottles and sponges while also giving them the opportunity to get messy and clean up. Some little ones shy away from using paint because they are uncomfortable with the mess, and this makes the mess a part of the experience as well as offering tools to clean up the mess.

1. Gather toy cars, a bin, washable paint, sponges, and spray bottles.

2. Start by letting your child get the cars dirty! Have them paint the cars with washable paint.

3. Once the cars are dirty, your little one can use the sponges and spray bottle to clean them up. The bin will contain the mess and can enrich the play; try adding some soap or shaving cream to extend the play.

Grown-Up Tip: You can also head outside with your cars to get them dirty while playing, or bring a bit of mud inside to use!

11

Train Station

All aboard! Trains are one of our favorite ways to travel, and in this chapter we are going to help you recreate that experience for your child. Create a map of a route, decorate their luggage tags, punch train tickets, and even make their own train whistle. Pretending to travel is a wonderful way for children to think about the world around them; they can imagine they are going to a familiar place or one they have never been to. Both scenarios are beneficial as your child is trying to figure out where they fit in the world, both literally and figuratively. Traveling can also be one of those activities that causes children anxiety, as there is a lot of activity, rules to follow, and plenty of unknowns, especially when going to a new place. Creating a scenario where they can get ready for their travels or reflect on them after returning can be beneficial in working through those feelings.

TOOLS FOR PLAY

- Wooden crates
- Small suitcases/bags
- Construction paper
- Markers and/or paint
- Tape
- 9 paper or plastic plates
- Cardboard
- Velcro tape (optional)
- Washi tape
- Scissors
- Foam board
- Silver duct tape
- Glue
- Cardstock
- Poster board
- White crayon or chalk
- Envelopes
- Hole punches of various sizes and shapes
- Toilet paper tubes
- Wax paper

Plastic plates

Wooden crates

Hole punches

Cardboard

TRAIN STATION

The train station has three areas where your little one can play and explore, the baggage claim and ticket counter inside the station and the train itself.

BAGGAGE CLAIM AREA

Stack a few crates to create the baggage claim, where you can place small pieces of luggage, such as toy suitcases or carry-on bags, or you could even make your own suitcases out of cardboard boxes and attach cardboard handles. Create a sign by drawing a simple suitcase on a piece of construction paper and tape it to the crates.

TICKET COUNTER

Stack a few crates to make the ticket counter. Draw a ticket on a piece of construction paper and tape it to the crates. You can add the cardboard computer from the doctor's office chapter to the counter! Add tickets made out of cardstock for your little one to sell.

TRAIN

Use three wooden crates to create a train. Place one upright on its short end to be the engine. Attach a steering wheel made out of a paper plate to the back. Right behind the engine place a crate for the engineer to sit in. Put the third crate behind the second, attaching the two with a piece of cardboard, or use small pieces of Velcro tape so that your little conductor can couple and uncouple the two cars. Take eight paper plates, draw spokes around the edges, and tape them to the sides of the train cars, two on each side of the car.

TRACKS

Use washi tape to create train tracks on the floor: tape down two long pieces of tape parallel to each other, approximately the same width apart as the train cars. Add shorter pieces of tape going across, leaving enough space between the short pieces for your little one to stand in the squares created.

SIGNS

Make a railroad crossing sign. Use two rectangles of foam board and wrap the short ends with silver duct tape. Glue them together to make an X. Make lights to go below with circles cut out of black and red cardstock. Make the red circles slightly smaller than the black ones and glue them on top so the black border shows all the way around. Take a small strip of foam board and glue a light on each end. You can tape these to the wall, or use a small wooden stand like the kind that comes with a housekeeping dramatic play set.

Make a departures and arrivals board by gluing pictures of different colored trains on a piece of poster board, leaving space to write the times next to each train. You can make the sign interactive by using a black poster board and writing the number with chalk, wiping it off to write new ones, or using index cards with times written on them and attaching them to the sign with Velcro.

BUILD A TRAIN MAP ROUTE

Maps are great for children to explore and allow them to develop their spatial thinking skills. For this activity you can work with your child to create a map of a real place, such as your street or the route to a favorite place and add the buildings you see along the way, or you can make an imaginary place for them to explore.

Extend the Play: You can use the tickets from the ticket punch activity later in this chapter; make your tickets in corresponding colors to the buildings and your little one can match the colors and slip the right ticket in each envelope.

1. Use a large piece of black construction paper for a small map or poster board to make a bigger map.

2. Use a white crayon or chalk to draw your tracks, leaving space on either side for your buildings.

3. Make the buildings with envelopes using a variety of sizes and colors; leave the top flap open to be the roof and add details with markers. Glue them down along the train tracks, making sure to leave the open side of the envelope facing out.

4. Your little one can drive their toy trains down the track.

MAKE YOUR OWN LUGGAGE TAGS

These luggage tags are a fun way for your little one to add some flair to their suitcases. Using the same colors of paper that you do for the tickets is also a great way to practice matching and color identification: your little one can make sure that each ticket holder also has a piece of luggage.

1. Cut strips of paper approximately 2 inches (5 cm) wide and set them out with a hole punch for your little one to use to punch out shapes. You can use a variety of shape punches or just the standard circle.

2. Once the strips are decorated, your little one can attach them to the luggage by looping them through the handles and gluing the ends together.

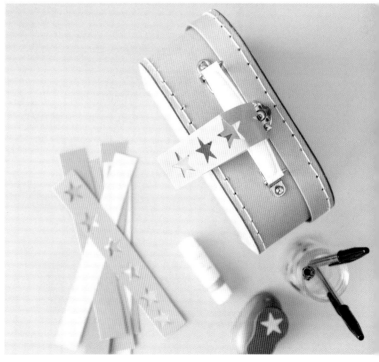

Grown-Up Tip: Thicker paper, like cardstock, will be easier for children to manage, as it will not be as floppy so they can focus more on punching the hole and less on managing the paper.

PRACTICE PUNCHING TICKETS

Hole punches are a fun way to work on those fine motor skills, and using different shape hole punches or craft punches adds a little more interest to the activity. You can also save the punched-out shapes and add them to a sensory bin or use in mixed-media art!

1. Cut tickets out of cardstock; you can get two or three out of each piece. Cut the corners off, making the cuts rounded.

2. Give the tickets to your child along with craft punches for them to use to punch shapes out of the tickets.

MAKE TRAIN WHISTLES

Making your own instruments is a fun way to explore with sound. Older children can get a closer look at how vibrations make sounds and use that knowledge to experiment with their instruments. For all children it is a simple way to explore cause and effect and start flexing those scientific thinking skills.

Age Adaptations: Older children can also write on the tickets, adding destinations, times, or prices to practice different skills.

1. Have your little one paint a toilet paper tube however they would like. Let it dry.

2. Poke a hole near one end of the roll. On that same end, secure a square of wax paper over the opening of the tube. Make sure you don't cover the hole.

3. Show your little one how to hum into the open end of the tube to make a sound. They can experiment with how far away from their mouth to hold the whistle and what sounds they can make.

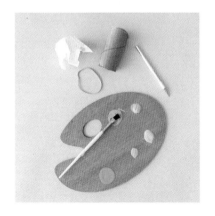

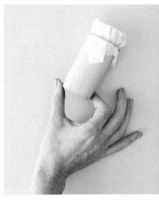

GROSS MOTOR TRAIN TRACK ACTIVITY

We often think of running and playing outside as how our children gain gross motor skills, but with a little creativity you can also work on those skills inside, especially when the weather is not cooperating for getting outside to play. It can also be a way to help inspire your child's play at the pretend train station setup. You can talk about places to take the train and familiarize them with vocabulary that they can use, such as "platform," "junction," and "route."

1. Have your child move along the train tracks in different ways; for example, they can tiptoe along one rail, hop from tie to tie, hop on two feet or one foot, take giant steps, take tiny steps, army crawl, or anything else you can think of.

2. To make this a more independent activity, you can make cards with simple instructions or pictures for your child to use. A fun twist is to tape the cards to a small box, such as a square tissue box, to use as a die your little one can roll.

Extend the Play: You can add a small suitcase to this activity for your little one to pull along the tracks. Placing heavy items inside the suitcase can increase the sensory input and make it a bit more challenging.

SKILL SHOUT-OUT

Gross motor skills allow your child to move smoothly through space, and by asking them to move in a variety of ways, they are strengthening muscles as well as gaining confidence in their bodies.

12

PRETEND PLAY

Toy Store

What kid doesn't love a trip to the toy store? In this chapter we are bringing the toy store to you, with a special twist. Our store has plenty of toys for sorting, pricing, and selling, allowing your little one to practice all those math skills as they play. But it also has a gift-wrapping center, so your child can work on their social and emotional skills as well, taking the perspective of others to select the perfect toy to be a gift. Additionally, wrapping those gifts is a fun way for your little one to start comparing sizes and volumes, working on distinguishing which container or sheet of paper will work the best for the size of toy they are trying to wrap.

TOOLS FOR PLAY

- Wooden crates
- Variety of toys
- Cardstock
- String
- Cash register
- Gift bags
- Toilet paper tube
- Long strip of paper
- Dowel, piece of string, or even a pipe cleaner

- Pencil, pen, or marker
- Paint and paintbrush
- Wire baskets
- Duct tape
- Wrapping paper
- Ribbon
- Tape
- Bows
- Brad

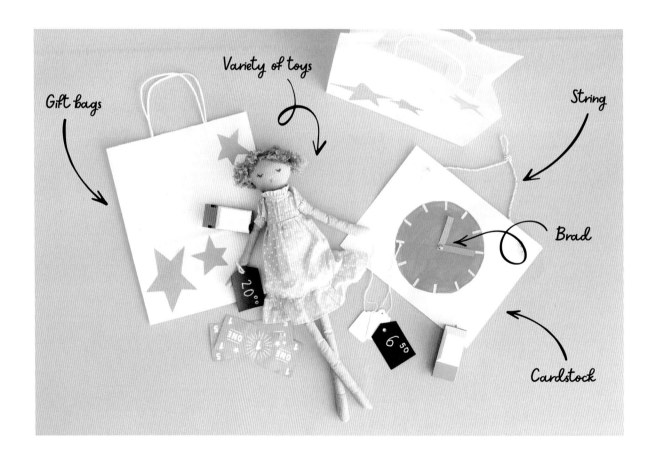

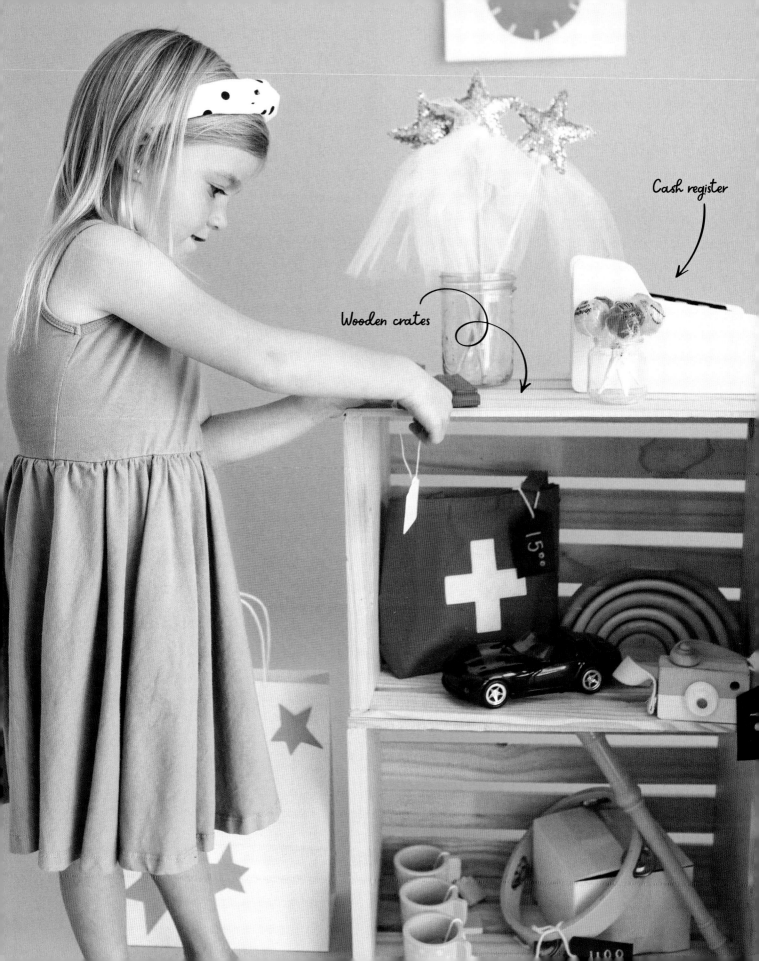

Cash register

Wooden crates

15⁰⁰

TOY STORE

Your toy shop needs shelves of toys, a counter where the cashier can sell the toys, and an area for gift wrapping.

- Create your shelves by stacking wooden crates and fill them with an assortment of toys.

- Add price tags to each toy by tying small pieces of paper to each one with a bit of string. You can also use dot stickers if you like.

- Put a cash register on top of the crates and add some plain gift bags for when customers check out.

RECEIPT WRITING ACTIVITY

Getting a receipt is how we end most of our shopping transactions, and creating that receipt is a wonderful opportunity to enrich this imaginative play setup. Finding ways to fold writing into imaginative play that make sense and feel natural can encourage early writing. Learning proper letter and number formation is important, but it can often feel like work and you end up with a result that is either right or wrong, which can be intimidating for some children who want to get it right. Writing a receipt puts the focus on creating an item for play, not on whether or not your numbers are written correctly, so it takes the pressure off while still allowing that exposure and experience.

1. Make a receipt roll. Take an empty toilet paper tube and a long strip of paper a little bit shorter than the tube.

2. Tape the end of the paper to the tube and wrap it around the tube until it is all wrapped up.

3. Slip the tube on a dowel, piece of string, or even a pipe cleaner and tape the ends down. This will keep the tube in place, but allow it to spin and let the paper unroll.

4. Add a pencil, pen, or marker and let your little one write the prices of the toys on the paper as their customers buy them.

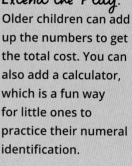

Extend the Play: Older children can add up the numbers to get the total cost. You can also add a calculator, which is a fun way for little ones to practice their numeral identification.

Grown-Up Tip: You can buy rolls of calculator paper at office supply stores, but they often come in rolls of 100 feet, which is tricky for children to manage. Taking a few feet from the roll and making this smaller roll makes it a lot easier. We look for plain paper rolls, not the thermal paper that is also available, as it is easier to write on. Or just cut a few pieces of plain white paper into strips and tape them together.

MAKE A SHOPPING BASKET

Your customers will need something to place their purchases in while they browse the toy shop and these baskets are perfect. It is often the small details, like a shopping basket, that really make an imaginative play setup feel realistic.

1. Take a small wire basket and a long piece of duct tape. Fold the duct tape in half so the sticky side is no longer exposed.

2. Use additional tape to secure the handle to the top of the basket. You can add a second handle if needed depending on the size of your basket.

SET UP A GIFT-WRAPPING STATION

Wrapping the toys adds an extra element to this shopping experience! It can also help open up conversations around holidays and birthdays when little ones may still be figuring out the rules of gift giving; for example, when an older sibling gets birthday presents it can bring up some confused feelings for the younger sibling about why they don't get anything and when it is their turn for presents. The shift from thinking about what you want to get to what you can give someone can be tricky for young children who are not as practiced at taking the perspective of others, and this activity lets them explore that shift.

1. Gather a variety of gift-wrapping materials, such as wrapping paper, ribbons, tape, bows, and gift bags. You can use up scraps you already have or purchase new items.

2. Cut the wrapping paper into various sizes of rectangles. You can also precut the ribbon into a variety of lengths if desired.

3. Place the items in a box or crate and allow your child to use them to wrap the toys in the toy shop.

4. You can also let your child decorate plain white paper shopping bags; older children may enjoy creating a logo for their shop!

Grown-Up Tip: If your child is getting frustrated with the ribbon, you can use wired ribbon to make it easier, just be sure to wrap up the ends with a bit of tape so the wire doesn't poke them!

Extend the Play: Your child can create their own wrapping paper to use by painting or drawing on pieces of kraft paper. Once dry, the kraft paper will be sturdy enough to use and reuse when wrapping.

OPENING AND CLOSING TIME ACTIVITY

Interactive signs are always a fun addition to an imaginative play setup, and this one has the added benefit of familiarizing your little with an analog clock, which is not as common as they once were. We kept it simple with just a clock, but feel free to add a second element where you have a list of days and times showing when the shop is open and closed.

1. Paint a large circle on the center of a piece of cardstock. Add twelve small bits of washi tape around the edge of the circle to mark the hours on the clock.

2. Cut out two strips of cardstock, making them a bit shorter than the radius of the circle. Punch a hole in the end of each. Attach them to the center of the clockface with a brad.

3. Punch holes in the top corners of the cardstock and attach a string so that the clock can hang.

4. Your little one can move the hands of the clock to show when the store is open and closed.

Age Adaptations: Older children can practice setting actual times with the clock. Making the two hands different colors to distinguish between the minute hand and the hour hand can be helpful.

Grown-Up Tip: If your child enjoys this activity, feel free to hang up the clock in your other imaginative play setups!

Acknowledgments

A heartfelt thank you to all of those who have shared and supported us in making this dream of writing a book come true.

To our husbands: JD, Austin, and Tre—this would not have been possible without your unwavering support. From taking the kids while we hid away writing and creating to cheering us on every deadline along the way, thank you for sticking by our sides even as we covered our homes with piles of crafts and supplies everywhere. Thank you for "tolerating" the glitter.

To our children: Brody, Isla, Luca, Piper, Flora, Alice, and Zooey—you are our inspiration for every activity we have ever created. Your willingness to be our test crew for each play scene, craft, and activity has helped bring joy to so many other families as well. You are our motivation to continue working hard. You are the magic in our lives.

To our parents: Thank you for making our own childhoods so magical. You taught us the importance of play and inspired our creative genes and passion for children that we've carried into adulthood.

To our Magic Playbook team: Brittany, Danielle, Brooke, Ashley, and JD—your dedication and all of the behind-the-scenes work you put in to keep Magic Playbook running smoothly while we spent over a year working on this book have been so appreciated. We wouldn't have been able to do this without you.

To our Magic Playbook community: Whether you have browsed our page for ideas, shared about Magic Playbook with a friend, been a subscriber, made a purchase from our shop, just stumbled upon us, or cheered us on from the sidelines from day 1, you are our motivation to keep creating. You have brought so much joy and purpose into our lives and we cannot thank you enough.

To those that made this book come to life: Jonathan Simcosky at Quarto, you believed in our idea and vision for this book from the beginning. Thank you for your support every step of the way. Raven Vasquez, we couldn't have asked for a more amazing photographer to capture the true magic of play. Your eye for angles and the way you work with children so naturally to capture these beautiful images are what have brought this entire book to life. Brittany Abney, our incredible graphic designer at Magic Playbook, thank you for your unending support and willingness to help with everything from mock-ups to doodles within the book. Your eye for design and color is impeccable, as is your understanding of our brand. Thank you for sharing your constant creativity with us; you never cease to blow us away with what you come up with. We are so lucky to have you on our team. And our adorable models, Bree, Dawson, Zen, Aria, Lane, Jrew, Lia, Hatley, Silas, Michael, and Charleigh, thank you for letting us capture your smiles and joy as you played.

Our immense gratitude,
Caitlin, Mandy, and Emma

About the Authors

Caitlin Kruse and Mandy Roberson are the cofounders of Magic Playbook, the original digital print-and-play kids' activities monthly subscription. Designed for ages two to six, Magic Playbook is an easy resource for parents to put together fun and seasonally appropriate activities for their kids and make everyday moments extraordinary. Their work has been featured in *Parents Magazine, Good Housekeeping, Buzzfeed, Daily Mom*, and many more.

With over a decade of content creation experience, Caitlin and Mandy have helped and inspired thousands of parents and caregivers through their kids craft and activity ideas. With their passions for sparking imagination in children, they have also launched and developed a line of products and toys under Magic Playbook that bring pretend play into homes across the world.

Emma Johnson joined the Magic Playbook team as their early childhood expert shortly after the brand launched and quickly became an integral part of the team. She holds a Master of Science degree in Early Childhood Education from Portland State University, with an infant and toddler mental health specialization, and has taught young children for ten years. Her work with Magic Playbook has helped set the foundation for lifelong learning in the homes of thousands of children.

Caitlin, Mandy, and Emma have a shared passion for bringing pretend play and easy activities into the homes of all. They hope this book will inspire you and your little ones to have fun playing!

Magicplaybook.com
@themagicplaybook

CAITLIN KRUSE

MANDY ROBERSON

EMMA JOHNSON

Index